AF575007

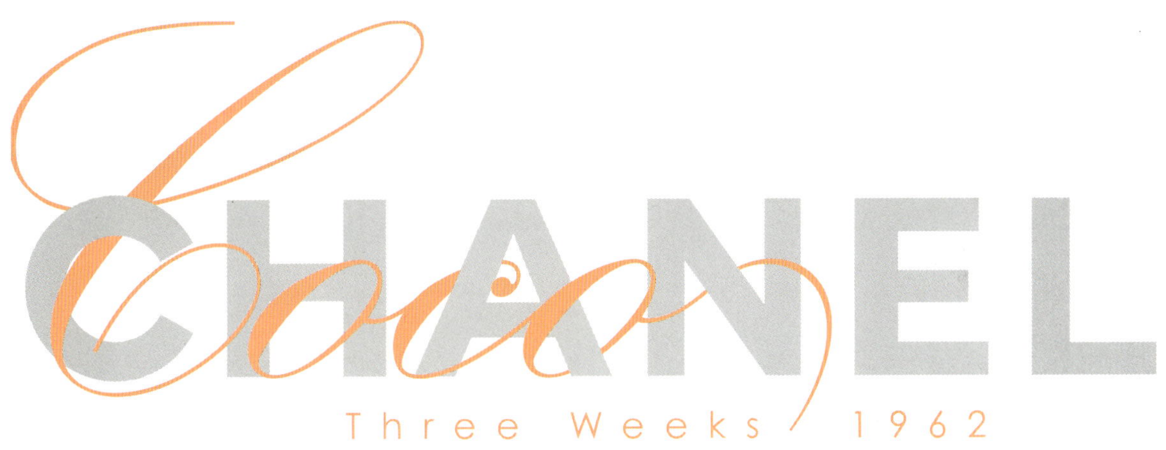
Coco
CHANEL
Three Weeks 1962

First published in the United States of America in 2008 by

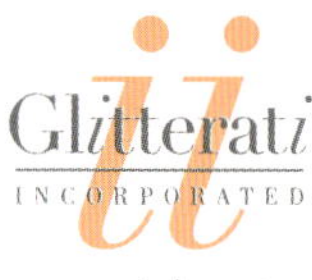


New York Office:
630 Ninth Avenue, Suite 603
New York, New York 10036
Telephone: 212 362 9119

London Office:
1 Rona Road
London NW3 2HY
Tel/Fax +44 (0) 207 362 9119

www.GlitteratiIncorporated.com
media@GlitteratiIncorporated.com for inquiries



First edition, 2008
Fourth Printing, 2015

Design: Sarah Morgan Karp/smk-design.com

Library of Congress Cataloging-in-Publication data is available from the publisher.

Hardcover ISBN 13: 978-0-9801557-1-6
Limited Edition ISBN 13: 978-0-9903808-2-5
Hardcover in French ISBN 13: 978-0-9862500-0-2
Limited Edition in French ISBN 13: 978-0-9862500-1-9

Printed and bound in China by Hong Kong Graphics & Printing Ltd.
10 9 8 7 6 5 4

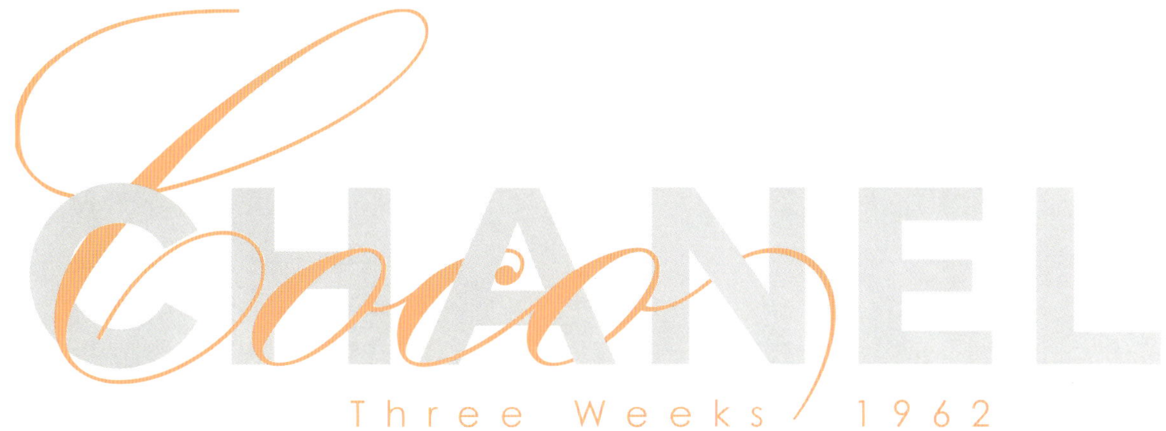


# Coco Chanel

## Three Weeks 1962



DOUGLAS KIRKLAND

With a foreword by Judith Thurman

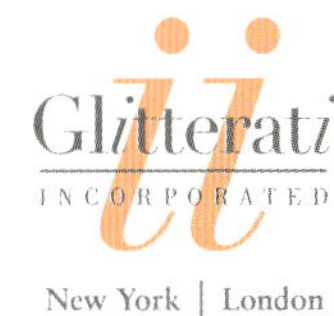

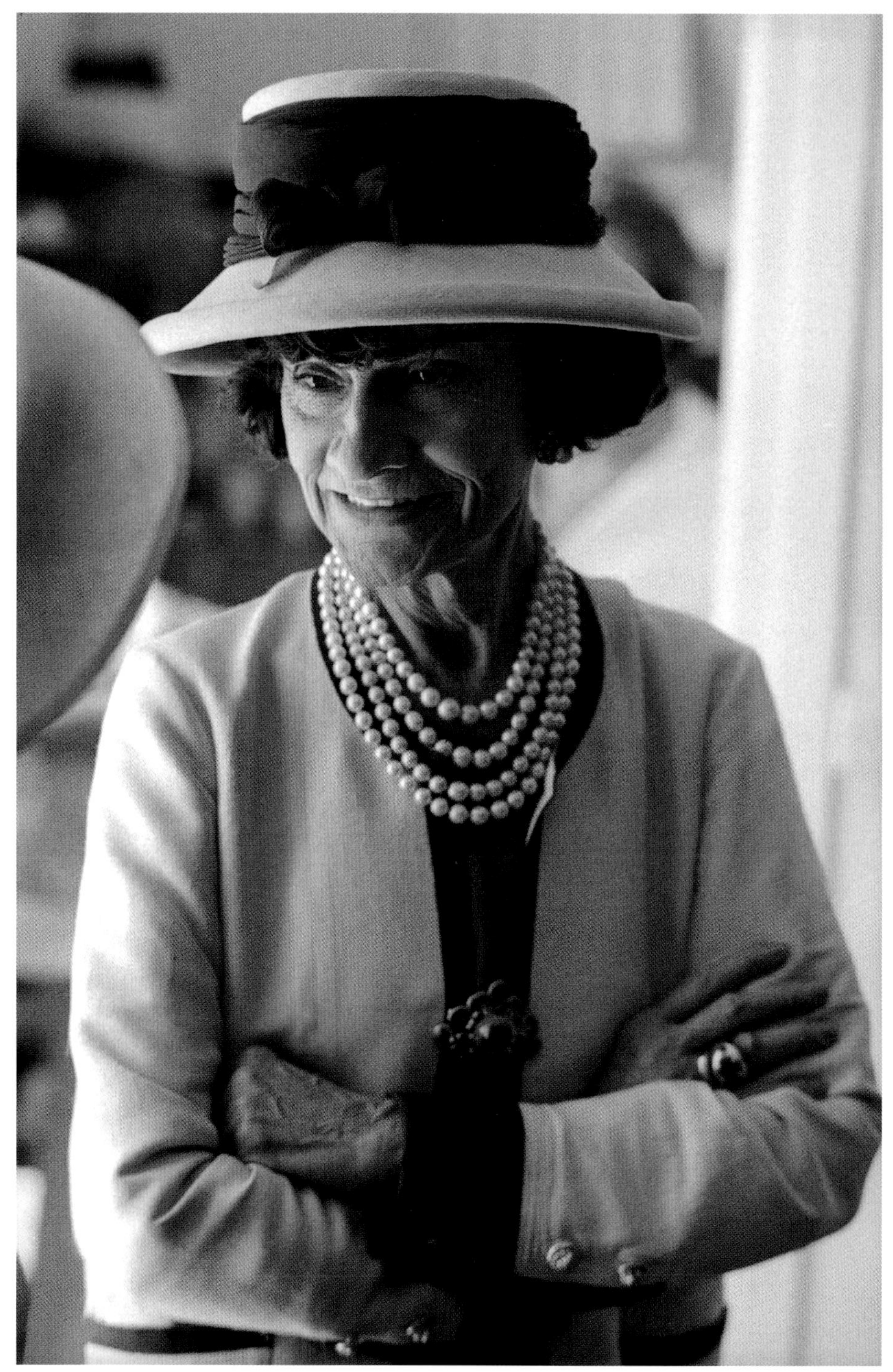

# Dedication

To Françoise

# FOREWord

They make an unlikely couple: innocence and experience.

He is twenty-seven, but he looks like a kid (a handsome kid) who has put a suit on for the first time.

She is seventy-nine, but she wears her wrinkles the way she wears her Chanel suit: with defiant elegance.

His smile withholds nothing. Hers suggests everything she knows—a lifetime of erotic wisdom—about withholding.

And yet Douglas Kirkland and Coco Chanel have something profound in common. Despite its rigor, their art is tender. It keeps faith with an ideal of beauty, which they refuse to fetishize. And they are both idealists about femininity. A woman of any age is safe in their hands.

"Safe" is not, generally, a compliment, either about photography or couture. It is a synonym for risk averse. A virtuoso never is, by definition, averse to a feat that tests his or her limits, and those of the possible. But that feat is also to make something daring or strenuous seem perfectly natural to a beholder anxious about his or her shortfalls of grace. It's a gift of buoyancy—of vicarious self-confidence. Great clothes give their wearers that gift, and the truth of a great portrait, however harsh it may seem at first glance, is ultimately uplifting since it reassures us that, whatever our differences, our kinship transcends them.

When the young photographer on his second trip abroad met the intimidating grande dame who, at first, ignored him, he could not have known that his career would be as long as hers (six decades, and in his case, still counting). Or that, five years shy of her age in these pictures, he would publish the photographs that he took in her atelier, and on the streets of Paris, forty-six years ago. He didn't yet know (or yet couldn't be sure) that time would reveal his incomparable talent for discerning the true colors of an elusive celebrity who had mastered the chameleon's trick of hiding in plain sight. But if you study the poignant encounter documented in this volume, you will discover why so many otherwise wary and artificial idols (Marilyn, Bardot, and countless others) have let down their guard. Chanel was a haughty, baroque character, and full of grudges. But her genius was for simplicity, and to achieve simplicity, you have to trust your instincts. That is what she saw—and trusted—in Douglas Kirkland. He shoots from the heart.

—Judith Thurman

In order to be *irreplaceable*
one must always be *different.*

CHANEL

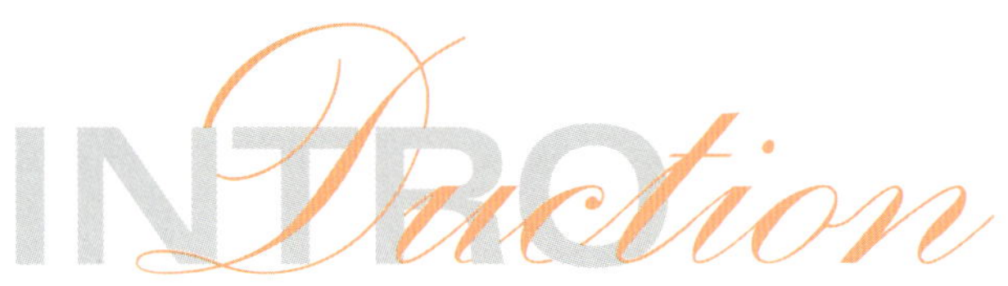


This is about who she was, who I was, and how she affected my life.

Paris, July 1962: when all self-respecting Parisians were off on holiday.

I watched Coco Chanel as she approached the atelier, marching energetically down the rue Cambon as she did every morning from her apartment at the Ritz Hotel, her home for more than twenty years. She was lost in her own world, hidden behind dark glasses—a very tiny woman who acted tall and gave off an aura of authority and certainty.

The formidable name "CHANEL" loomed above the atelier door. But I knew so little about her, and even less about Paris. I was a twenty-seven-year old photojournalist working for *Look Magazine*, and this was only my second trip here. The first time, I had worked mainly with Americans shooting a story about Art Buchwald of the *Herald Tribune*. I had stayed at the Hotel California on the rue de Berri, just off the Champs Elysées.

Now I was surrounded by French people, with the exception of my editor Pat Coffin, and was about to be ushered into the rarified world of haute couture. This was a vastly different Paris, imbued with more grandeur than the one I had observed on my first trip: the Place Vendôme, the rue Saint-Honoré, and the Place de la Concorde. The streets and the avenues were wide and glamorous, the shops exotic, the city of light sparkling, the nightlife mysterious. I felt a mixture of awe and uncertainty.

Looking back, I marvel at my lack of sophistication. My idea of fashion was Christian Dior's much talked about "New Look," which made headlines in 1947 with hemlines almost to the floor. Widely copied, it made its way to my native Canada via Eaton's catalog and fashion stories in *Life*, *Chatelaine*, and other publications that were all the rage with my mother and her style-conscious friends.

I was eager to learn all I could about Paris and the exciting world to which I was being admitted, although I did not speak French. No one seemed to understand English, and I had trouble communicating. When I left New York, it had been hot and humid, and although it was mid-summer, Paris was cool, gray, and rainy. I felt helpless about how to get around except by asking the doorman of my hotel, the Lotti, on the rue de Castiglione, to tell the taxi driver where I wanted to go.

I saw everything through small-town eyes. I had left Fort Erie, Ontario, Canada, population seventy-five hundred, only a few years earlier. In New York, as I struggled to build my career I had taught myself to walk, dress, and work with an air of complete confidence, but I secretly knew I was not as worldly as I was implying.

This was a completely unfamiliar environment, and I felt awkward and inadequate. The tiny cars on the streets were so different from the huge American dreamboats, with their masses of chrome. At the airport, I had to fold my six-foot-three frame into a small Peugeot taxi and stuff my bags into its miniscule trunk. On the boulevards the women glided by, sexy and chic. The men acted superior, sitting in cafés and puffing on their Gauloises. I wondered where they came from and what was going through their heads. Everything in the streets seemed to move very quickly, leaving me disoriented. At no time in my life have I learned so much so fast. I felt like a child learning to walk and talk.

Out of this experience came the pictures in this book.

## On the outside looking in: first impressions

Mademoiselle's hair was black under the hat I never once saw her remove. Her features were sharp and determined. "A woman has the age she deserves," she had proudly announced on more than one occasion. At seventy-nine, she still had impeccable posture and stood erect as a ballerina. She couldn't have weighed more than ninety pounds and moved around with great energy. Everyone always showed her total respect. She made opinionated statements, and I don't ever remember anyone disagreeing with her.

She ruled with complete control the fashion empire she had built. Since the close of the First World War, her modernist approach and menswear-inspired fashion had made her the symbol of emancipated female elegance. She introduced the black turtleneck sweater and trench coat and all black for evening. Her "little black dress" became popular for its versatility day or night. She pioneered short hair, short skirts, and low heels. As early as 1923, she told *Harper's Bazaar* that "simplicity is the essence of elegance." Chanel Number 5 (named after her lucky number), the perfume that made her a millionaire, became a household word.

Born on August 19, 1883 (she changed that date to 1893), in Saumur, France, about two hundred miles from Paris, Gabrielle Chanel came from humble beginnings. She learned to sew in the orphanages where she lived as a child. After a brief career in cabaret, in 1909 she transformed herself into "Coco" Chanel with the help of wealthy lovers who established her in a little millinery shop in Paris at 31 rue Cambon. On that street her couture house stands to this day.

Her beauty and her flair made her many interesting friends. Jean Cocteau, who lived in her house for a year, called her "my Little Black Swan." She financed a ballet for Diaghilev and greatly admired the painter Juan Gris. She could have married many times, but she treasured her independence. All her life she seemed to regard men as lovable ornaments.

Chanel's questionable behavior during the Second World War was subsequently hushed up. Her affair with a German officer, Hans Gunther von Dinklage, led to investigations after the liberation, but charges were dropped thanks to influential friends. Her past was always something she didn't really want to discuss and preferred to embellish.

After closing her shop in 1939, when she made her comeback in 1954, "it was as though she had been out to lunch," said one journalist. Rumor had it that she came back to boost her perfume sales, but she also wanted to show Paris couture how to design again. With a sarcastic smile she said, "Members of the third sex are not craftsmen. They make a drawing,

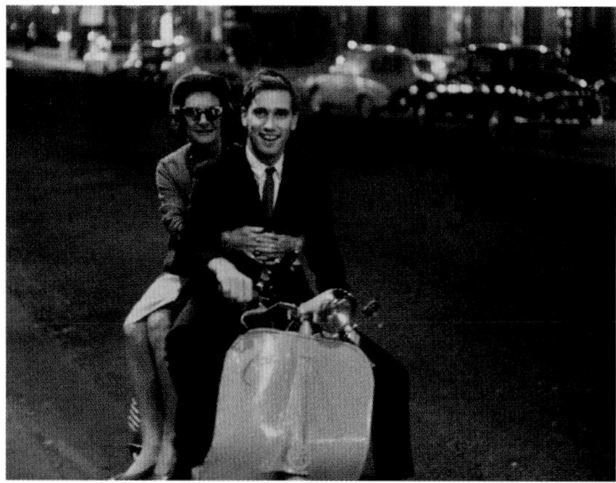

**Douglas Kirkland with *Look Magazine* Fashion Editor Patricia Coffin riding a rented Vespa, ". . . that Vespa I rented gave me the sense of being young and free in Paris."**

and it is copied for them. They play the guitar and entertain at cocktails. They hate the dresses they are making because they wish they could wear them. So they make them unwearable."

I could easily have not made the trip to Paris at all. There had been numerous disagreements in the editorial offices of *Look* in New York as to whether Chanel even justified a story. Some editors loved the idea; others hated it. Fashion editor Pat Coffin supported it because Chanel's designs had moved into the White House with Jacqueline Kennedy. Editor in Chief Dan Mich came from a sports background, knew nothing about fashion, and wanted to keep it that way.

Chanel had wanted a fashion spread, but the magazine asked me to deliver a reportage on her. Pat and I had been demoted to flying coach on this particular assignment, at a time long past, when photographers and journalists always traveled first class. This story just wasn't considered significant enough.

I gradually got comfortable, the rue de la Paix was becoming my stomping grounds, a long way from the Niagara Boulevard. I rented a Vespa for buzzing around the city and frequently got lost. The policemen still wore capes and white gloves when directing traffic. Going around the Etoile was a most daunting challenge. In my attempt at being French, I would order wine at lunch, feeling it was very sophisticated, but in the afternoon after sitting through endless interviews conducted in a sea of rapid French, which I didn't understand, I found myself feeling drowsy and desperately fighting sleep. I would walk each morning to the Chanel boutique with Simone Gauthier, *Look*'s Paris bureau chief and etiquette instructor for visiting *Look* staff. Her role consisted of everything from translating to acting as "best friend" to the wives and daughters of the management, to taking them out to buy gloves and scarves. On the way to the atelier, Simone often stopped at the corner bar for a quick coffee and occasional shot of brandy, which she'd consume in one gulp while standing at the counter. Simone represented the voice of wisdom and authority on all things French.

When I asked Simone why Chanel was called "Mademoiselle," she answered, "That's a delicate question. Normally a woman her age would be addressed as 'Madame,' whether married or not." But she said that Chanel, a fiercely independent woman, wanted to prove that she was above the system and didn't need marriage or a relationship to a man to be successful.

At first, Mademoiselle barely acknowledged me. I looked even younger than I was and was certainly not a known name. Before she would trust me, she insisted that I photograph some of her fashion, process the film, and make prints for her to see. As I was about to shoot the models wearing the latest Chanel creations, Pat Coffin told me to watch for the following: the square-cut classic Chanel suit, the shorter hemlines, the very popular quilted handbags with the identifying shoulder chain, the low-heel signature two-tone pumps, as well as the costume "junk" jewelry Chanel made acceptable for wealthy women to wear. Coco Chanel routinely mixed fake and real strands of pearls. Jewelers copied her designs. The Chanel look had become a classic, almost a cliché, but there was a public demand for it because of its simplicity, which made it so easy to copy. "I must be rich," Chanel joked, "the way people steal from me. Let them! Unless the whole world wears your clothes, you are not creating a fashion."

I worked spontaneously, following my instinct. My approach was very simple. I would choose the girl, and after she was dressed and made-up, I'd take her out to the location of my choice: the Place de la Concorde, the Tuilerie Gardens, or the Louvre—just myself, the model, and the clothes. I wasn't followed by a staff of assistants, stylists, or hair and makeup people. The models were friendly. In French, they were called "les mannequins," and they worked full time for the House of Chanel. They flirted with me and treated me like a little brother. Most everyone was very willing and anxious to help me since I represented the influential American publication of the day, *Look*.

Ignorant of the fact that Chanel had spent time in England and had almost become the duchess of Westminster, I assumed that, like many French people of the time, she didn't speak English. Then one morning I turned a corner in a narrow hallway at the atelier and found myself face–to-face with her. She looked straight at me and said, "Salut." I froze, not knowing how to respond. After a beat, in her low voice, she said in perfect English, "I just said hello to you."

From that moment on, Mademoiselle took a liking to me, and my work could finally get started. I had been given a green light, and I started spending long hours with Mademoiselle and her staff. Nothing was off-limits. "You must learn French," she frequently told me. "Learn a few words every day, sing songs, read the newspaper. And if you don't understand a word, look it up in your dictionary." This was the beginning of my love affair with Paris and the French, which eventually led to my marriage to Françoise a few years later.

## Moving into the inner circle

It is difficult to describe the excitement I felt as I watched Chanel create a new design, oblivious of everyone. She strived for perfection with scissors and pins, her hands nimbly working a sleeve or a lapel: "I sculpt what I design." The atelier was the creative nerve center. Once she started working, a beehive of assistants immediately surrounded her.

"The bustline is important—I want to see the girl underneath the fabric," Mademoiselle said. She never minded showing off a bit for the camera, and the attention the Americans were giving her pleased her. "Fashion has become a joke. The designers have forgotten that there are women inside the dresses. Most women dress for men and want to be admired. But they must also be able to move, to get into a car without bursting their seams! Clothes must have a natural shape."

As a photographer, your hands fall on the right places of your camera. The touch of the lens, the feel of the aperture have the comfort and intimacy one feels with a lover. You steer into where you find the image, the perfect frame. To this day, I still feel magnetically drawn as I start shooting. I run through a disciplined checklist: Am I keeping the camera steady? Is the exposure right and the focus? Am I at the best angle and in the right place? Should I be talking, yelling, or silent? As everything goes on, I must be listening as well as finding pictures. I must be sensitive to my subject. Those are the thoughts that kept running through my head, over and over as I was photographing around the atelier.

## The collections

As the *défilé* (show) approached, the sense of urgency in the air was palpable. Everyone started moving faster. "This dress needs to be pressed; this sleeve is wrong; too short; I don't like this hemline." There was growing tension everywhere in the workrooms. At the end of one long day, Mademoiselle sighed, "My hands are sick, they have worked too much."

She deplored what she saw as the passing of good craftsmanship. "What is not in good taste doesn't interest me. People say my collections are all the same, but they are not. Like that plant over there, a few tired leaves drop, but see the new ones? If I don't have a new leaf in every collection, I'll stop." (She was still working in 1971 at the time of her death.)

Finally in early August, the big day arrived. The models marched into the showrooms carrying numbers as a select group of journalists and clients watched: Claude Pompidou, soon to become first lady of France; English actress Rachel Roberts, wife of Rex Harrison; Princess Lee Radziwill, Jacqueline Kennedy's sister; Art Buchwald, the celebrated American columnist for the *International Herald Tribune*; and fashion editors and illustrators from all the major newspapers.

Mademoiselle was famous for sitting on the stairs and watching the crowd's reaction through the kaleidoscopic mirrors, without being seen. She'd set herself down with the ease and agility of a woman half her age.

This collection was another spectacular success—Organza evening dresses, gold and white; the classic Chanel look, her signature white silk camellia. As one fashion editor said, "She still makes others look as if they tried too hard." When it was over, there was a celebration in the main dressing room, where the sound of champagne being poured mixed with laughter and chatter.

When I recently watched the brilliant documentary *Lagerfeld Confidential*, I marveled at how radically the fashion shows have changed since Chanel's day. The gilded velvet-covered chairs and quiet sitting rooms have been replaced by the most eccentric venues, the elegant chandeliers with flashing spotlights. Backstage, models prance around in G-strings instead of white blouses, and the once-hushed audiences now behave more like fans at a rock concert.

After Simone and Pat went off on their vacations, I was left alone in Paris to finish the story. As Mademoiselle and I grew closer, I wondered if she thought of me as the son she never had, or some distant lover from her past. In an affectionate way she encouraged me to grow up and improve myself. She was fifty-two years older than I. As she lay on her sitting room sofa one afternoon, she showed me how she liked to sleep at night, on her stomach; her legs were those of a young woman.

Mademoiselle loved to gossip, and was in her element starting intrigues. She wore a man's watch, unlike the small ones seen on women's wrists at the time. She was always way ahead of everyone. One day she showed me the contents of her handbag, and I remember a stack of ten-franc notes ($2.00) she claimed to pass out as tips. This was quite surprising, considering she had a reputation for being stingy with her employees. A chain-smoker, she would light her filter cigarettes with a 1925 Dunhill lighter, a gift from a dear friend. "I prefer to keep mementos rather than photographs," she said. "I'm not frivolous, I am light as a bird—especially with those I love."

Her range of interests was as extraordinary as her vitality. She discussed her new venture: Having been a horseracing fan for years, she had decided to become an owner as well. "I want only a few, but I want the best," she said. Of course, as in everything she undertook, her intention was winning. Her racing color was to be beige.

## The end

I remember the last Saturday afternoon I spent with Chanel. We were going to Versailles but started at her apartment with lunch, where she gave me lessons in table manners. At the end of the meal, to my astonishment, she asked me if I'd like to go to Switzerland with her on vacation and make more pictures. I could barely contain my excitement. What an opportunity! I couldn't wait to contact my office in New York and be congratulated. The coverage would be even more complete, a photojournalist's dream.

The chauffeur drove, and I sat in the front looking back at her as we left the city. In an about an hour, we arrived at the Château de Versailles. My breath was taken away by the splendor, the magnificent alleys, the gardens and statues. As we walked, the summer day turned chilly and gray, and it eventually started to drizzle. I offered Mademoiselle my raincoat, which she put over her shoulders turning it into a stylish cape. As our time was ending, I looked back in the graying light and saw her small figure in the distance. I asked myself, "How could such a small individual command such power?" I raised my camera quietly and made one final photo, which is my lasting vision of Coco Chanel.

When I walked into the *Look* office on Monday, the response to my scoop of Mademoiselle in Switzerland was waiting on the telex. Two words: "COME HOME!"

It was over. But the young man who left Paris a few days later was vastly different from the boy who had arrived. Almost fifty years and many experiences later, I still hear her words urging me forward.

—Douglas Kirkland

Elegance is not the prerogative of those who have just escaped from adolescence, but of those who have already taken possession of their future.

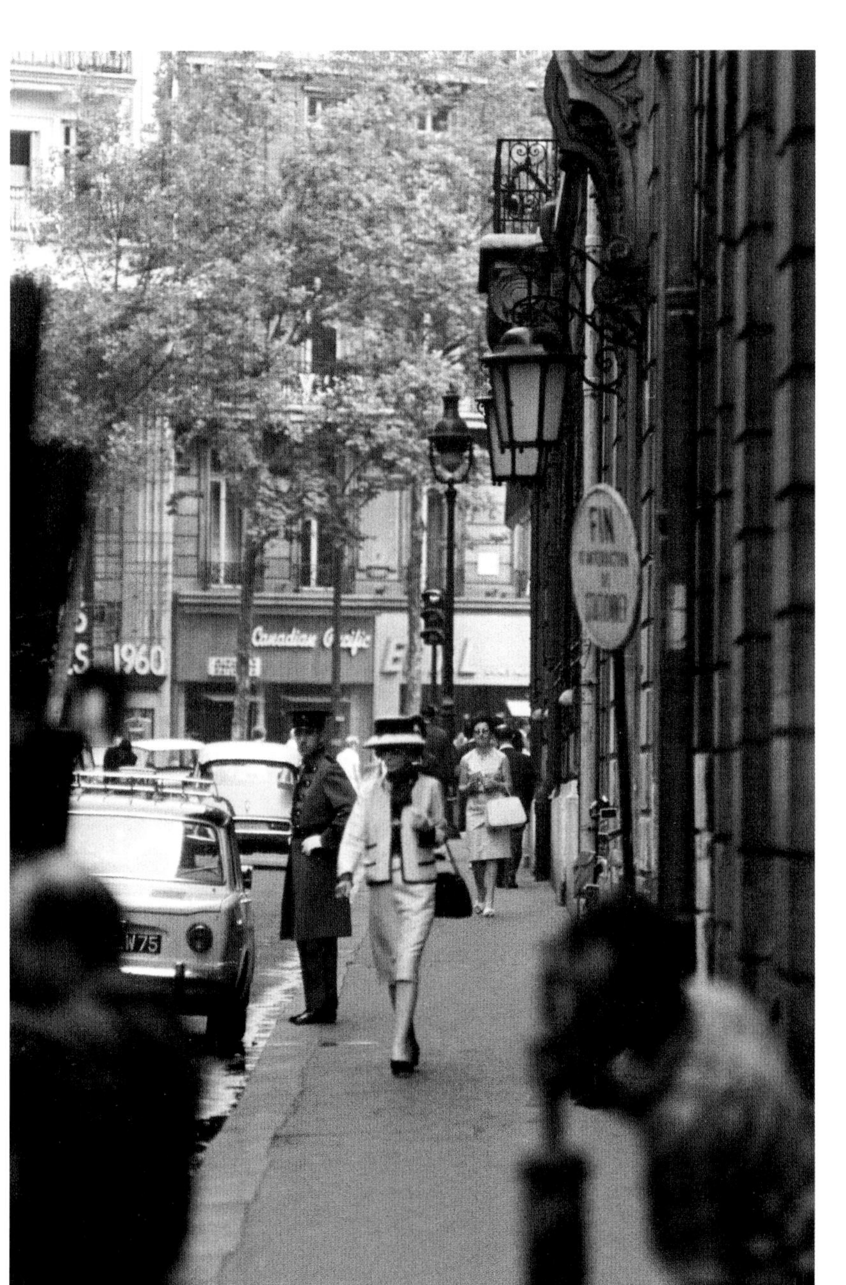
1960
Canadian
FIN

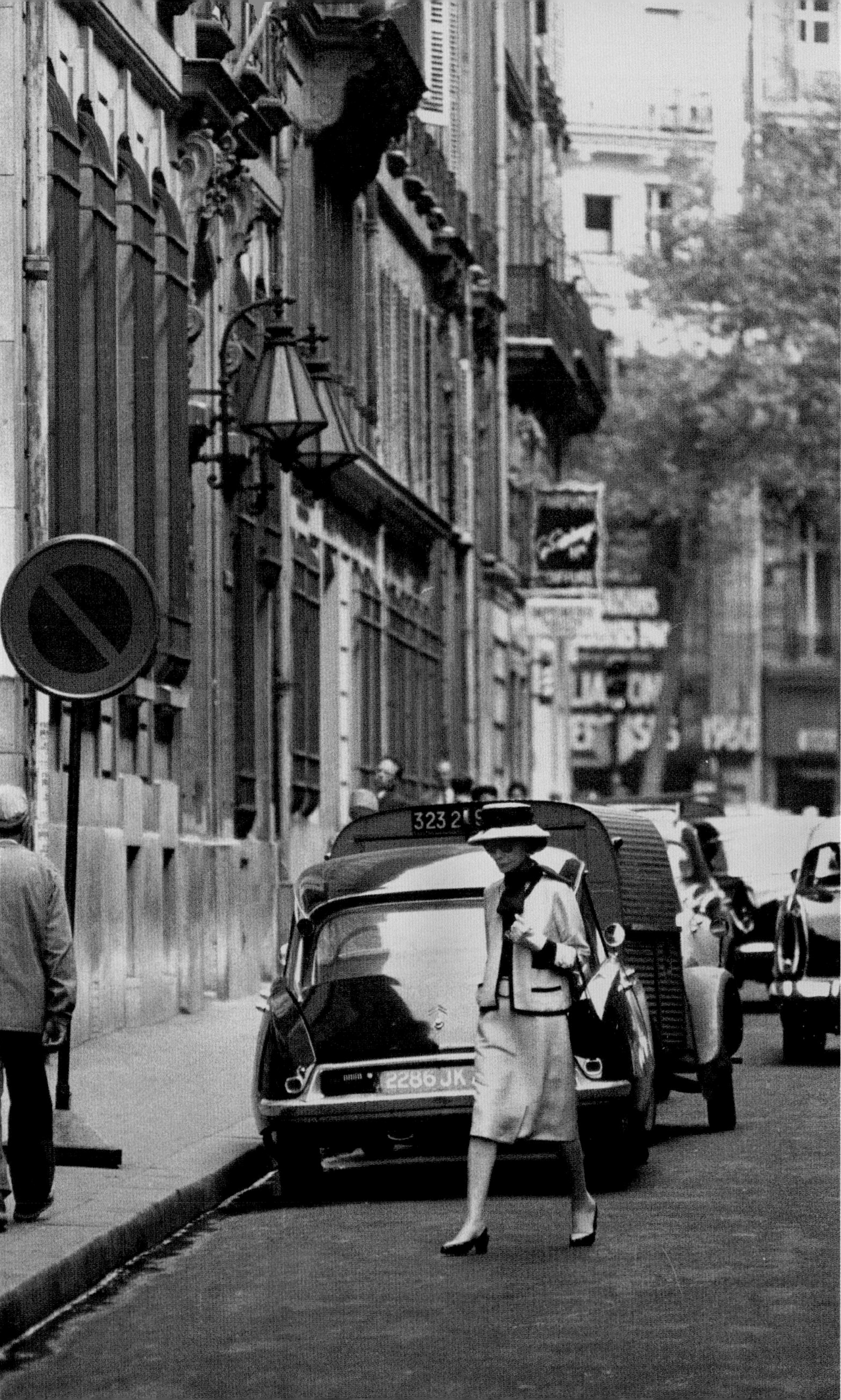
2286 JK

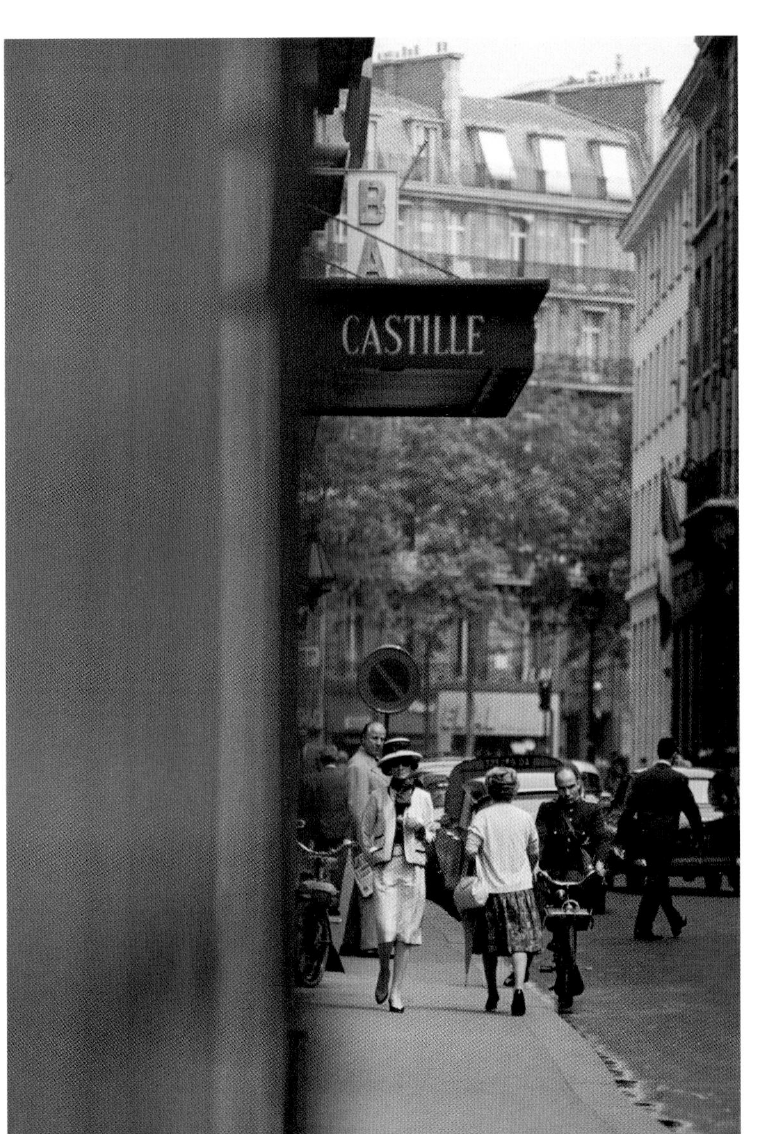
CASTILLE

At first, I didn't get close to Mademoiselle,

I observed her from a distance.

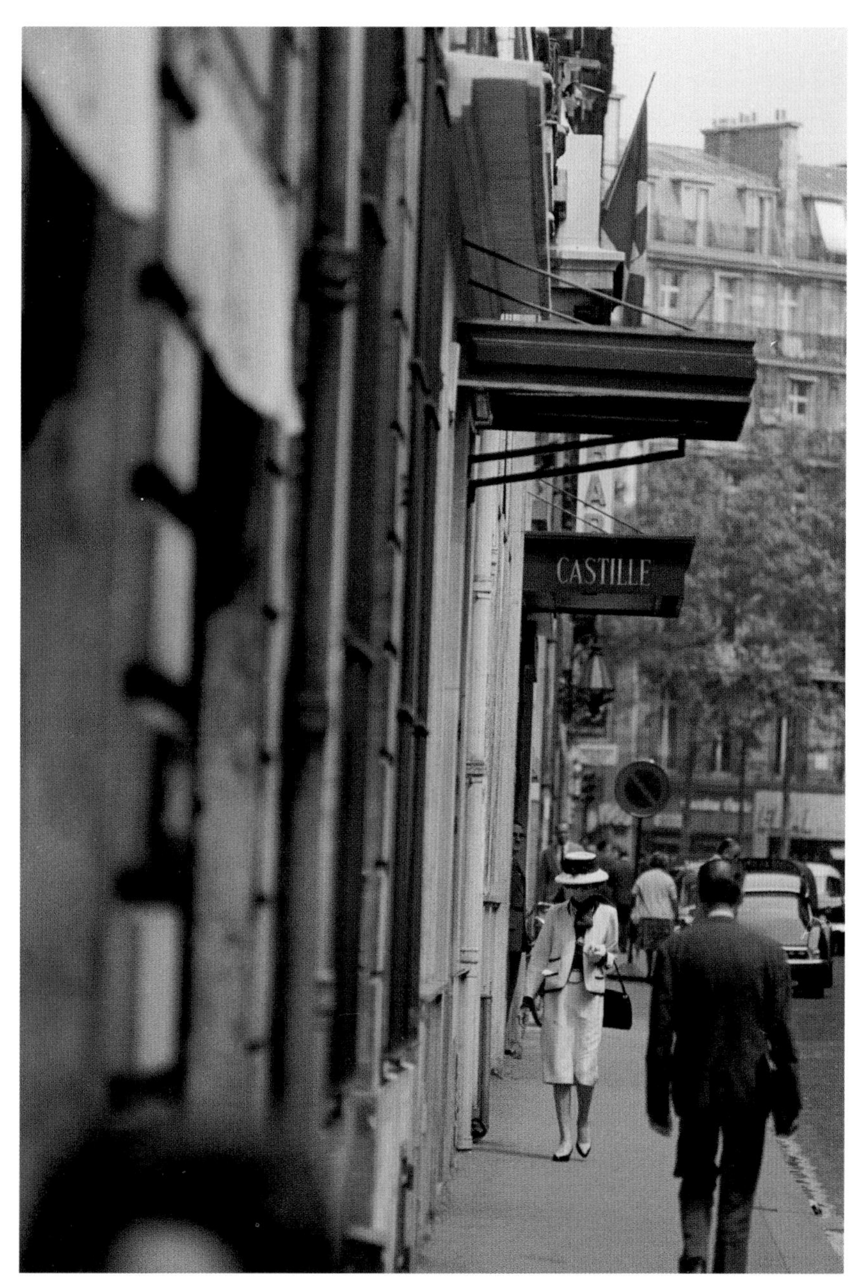
CASTILLE

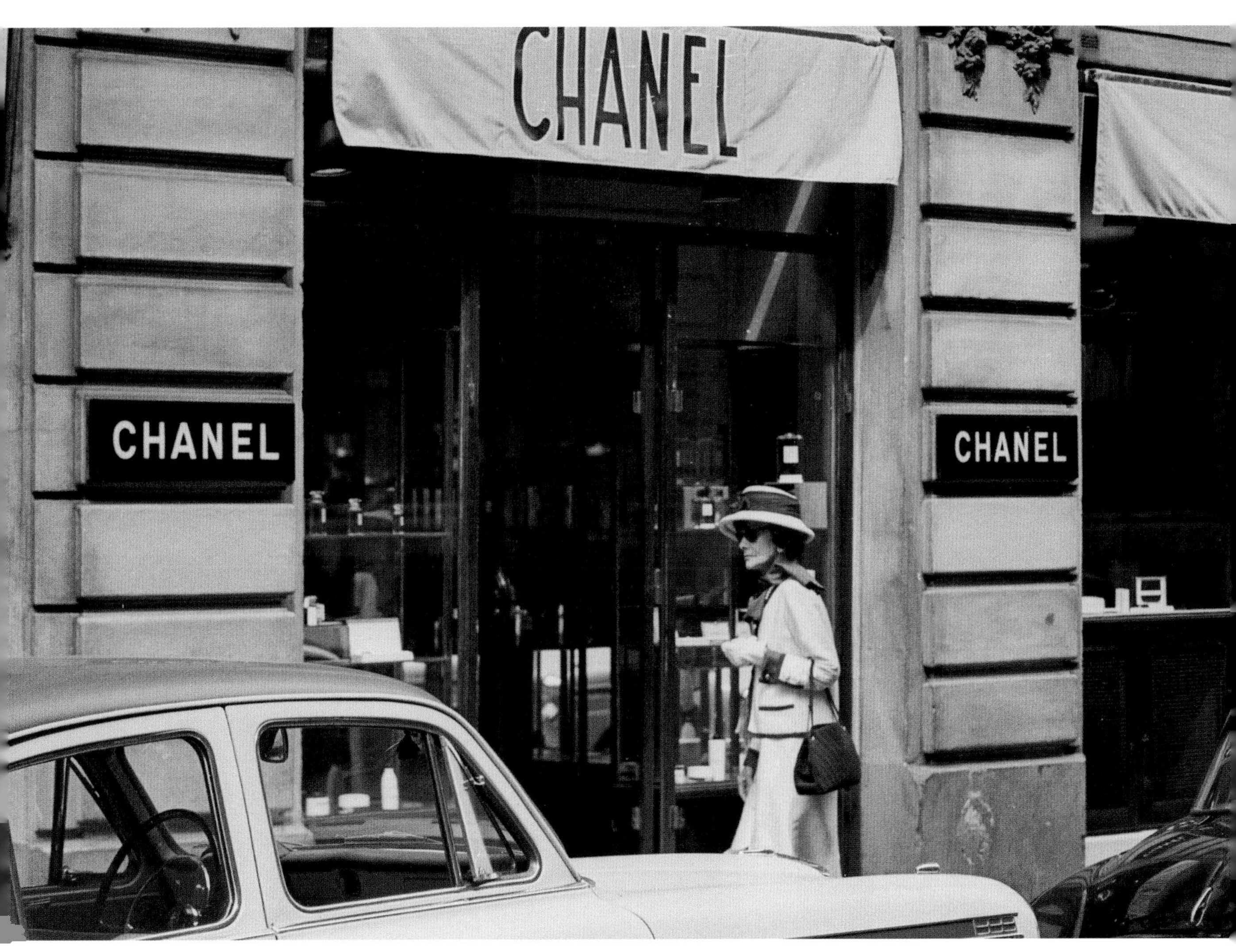
CHANEL
CHANEL
CHANEL

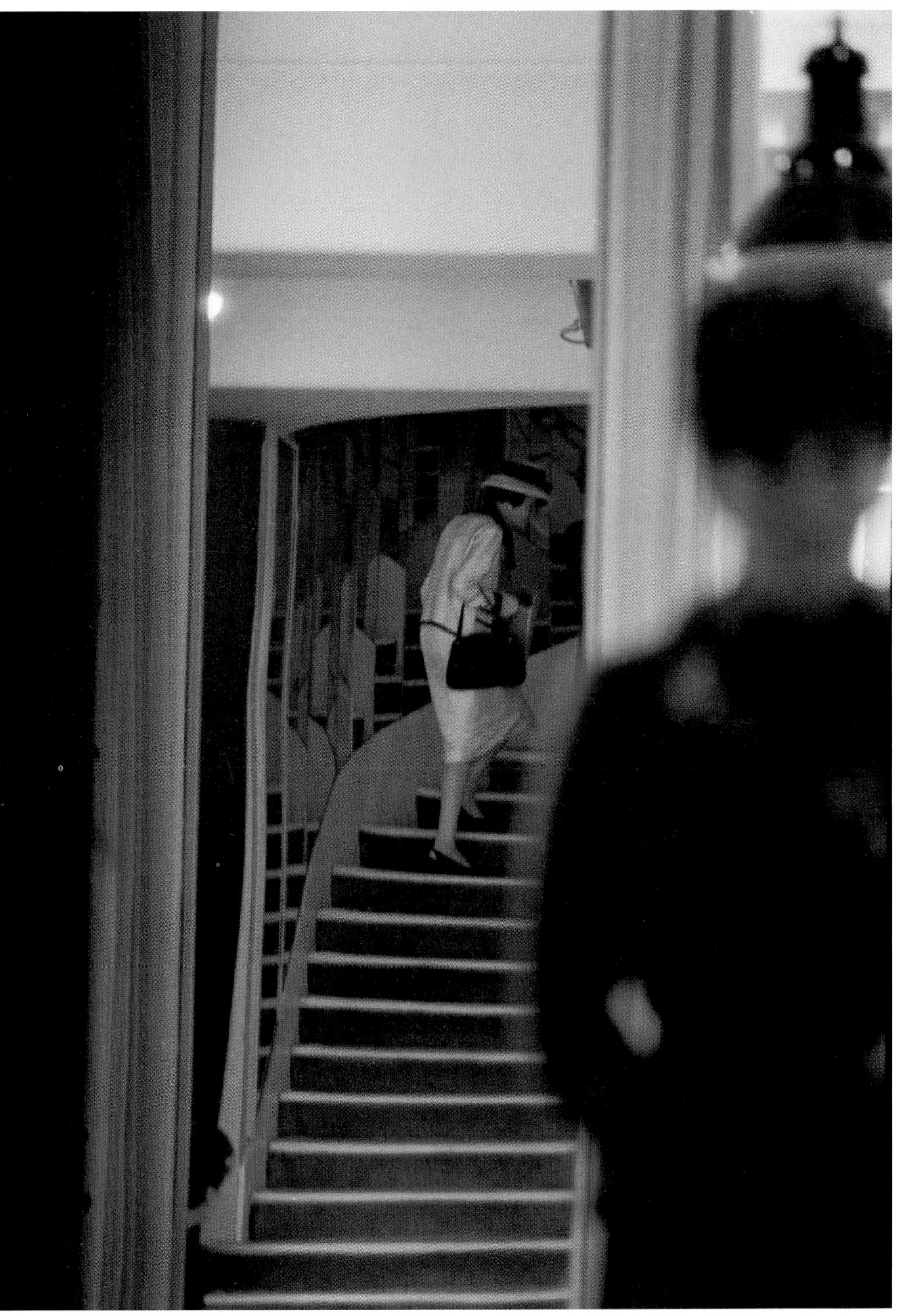

Fashion is not something that exists in dresses only. Fashion is in the sky, in the street, fashion has to do with ideas, the way we live, what is happening.

The signature quilted Chanel bag was as coveted in the early '60s as it is today.

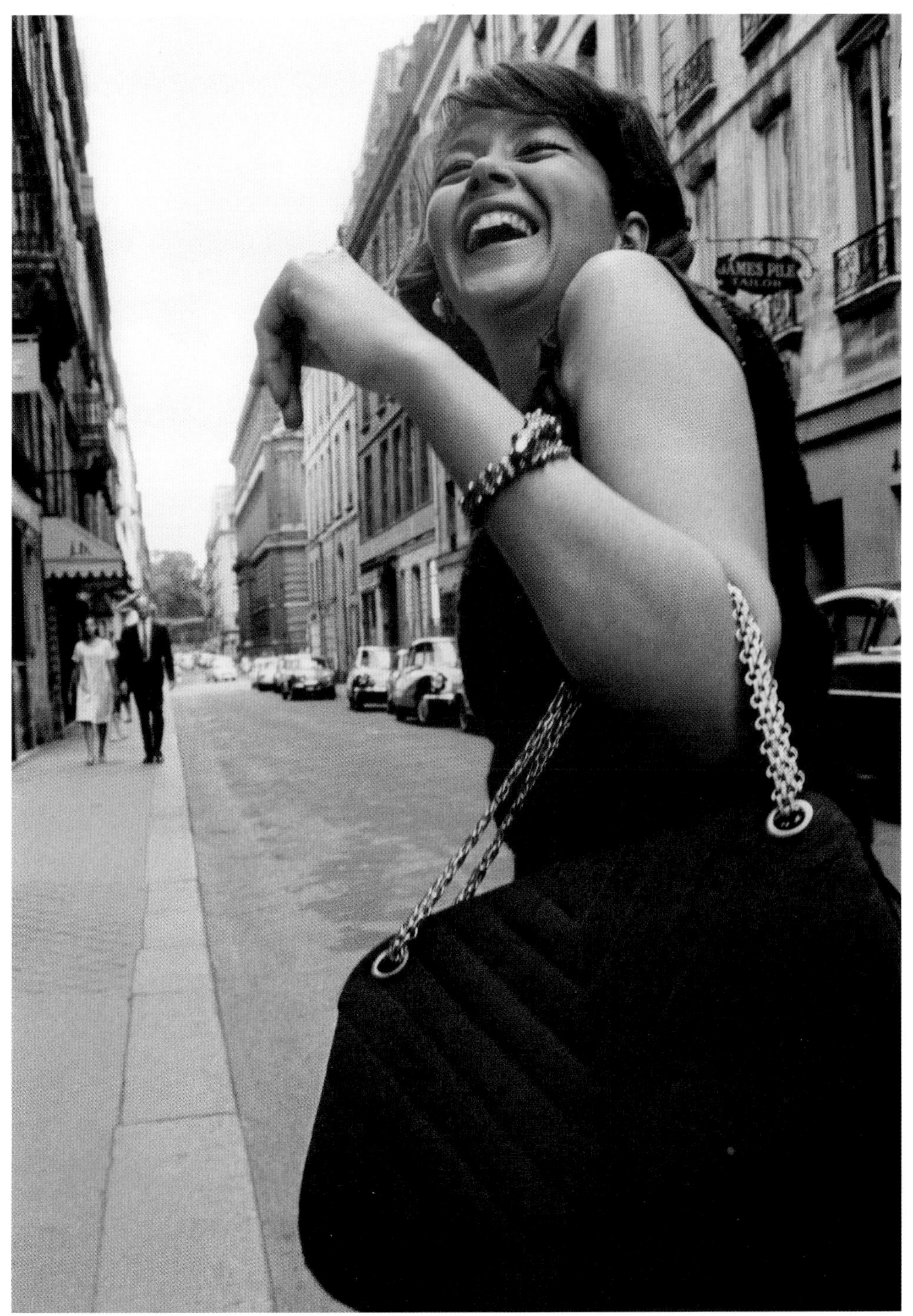
JAMES PILE
TAILOR

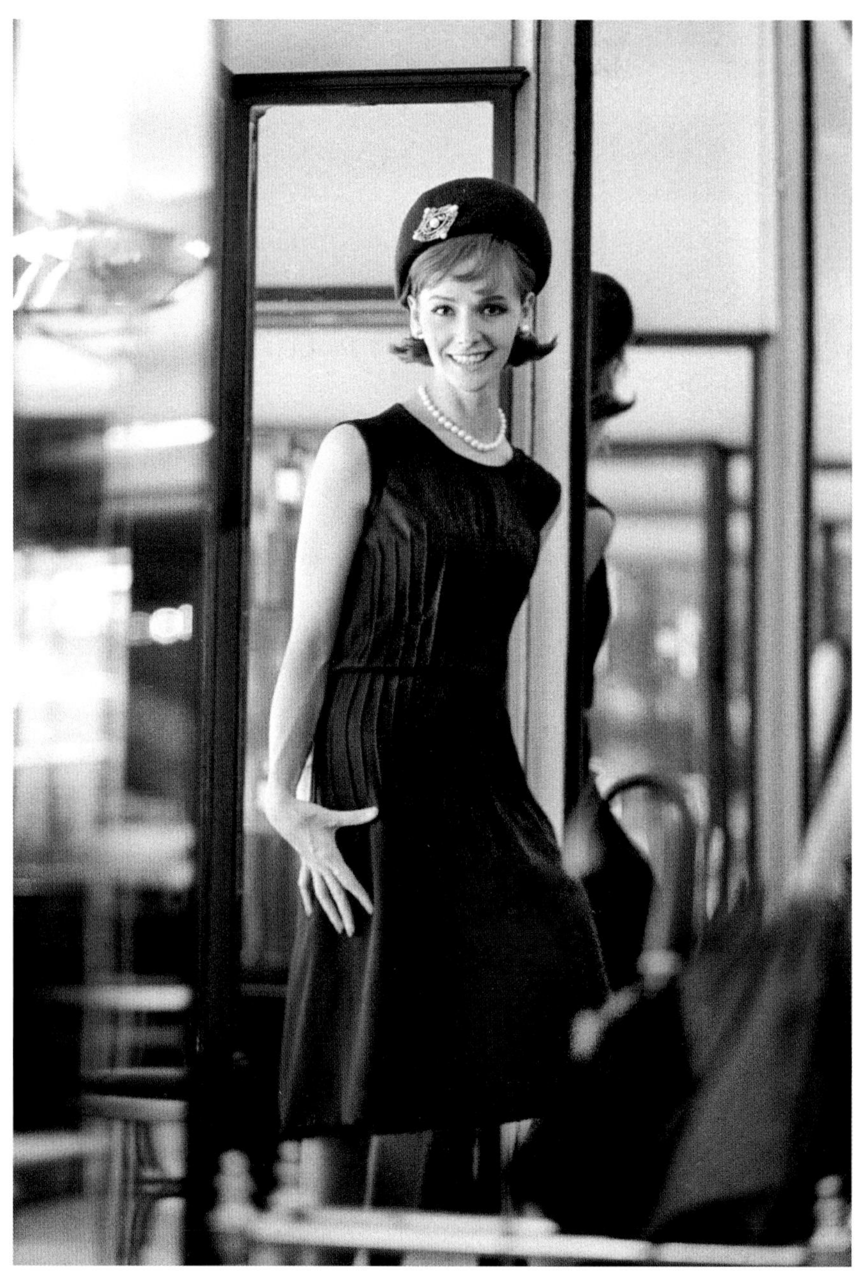

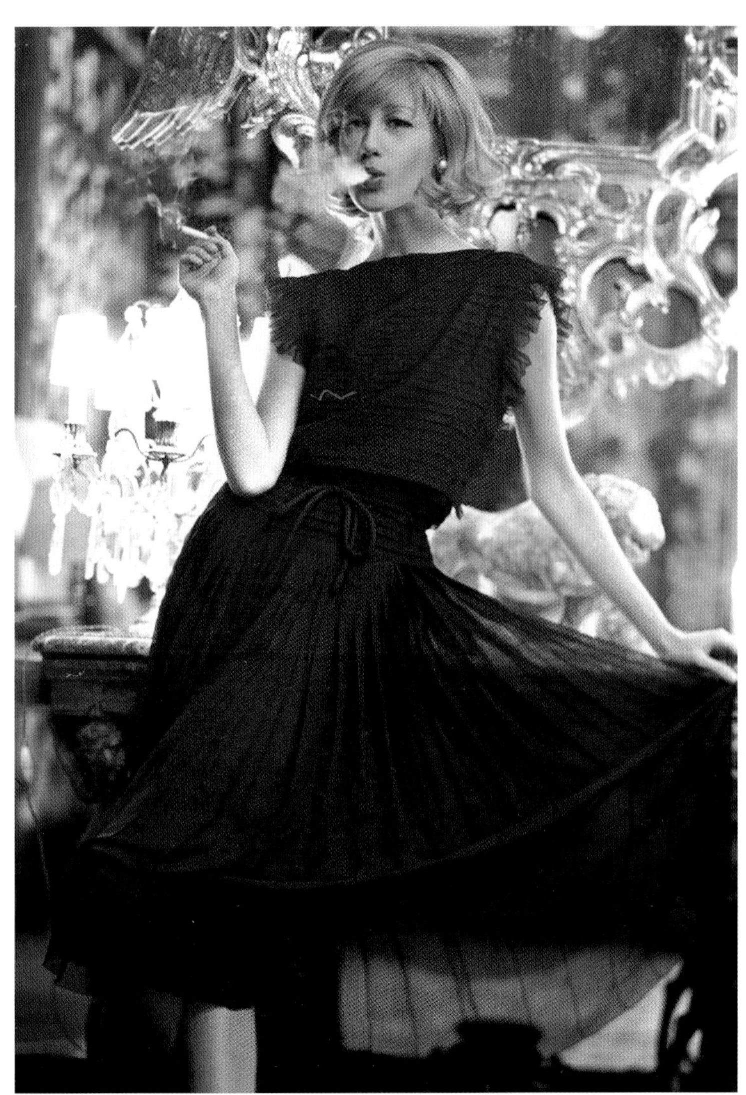

I shot some fashion to please Mademoiselle but had to have the film developed in Paris to show her before she would trust me.

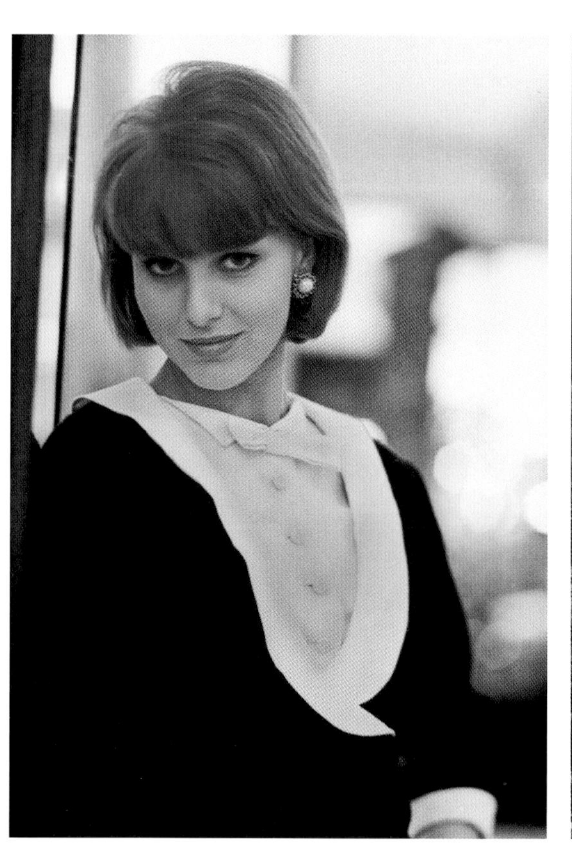

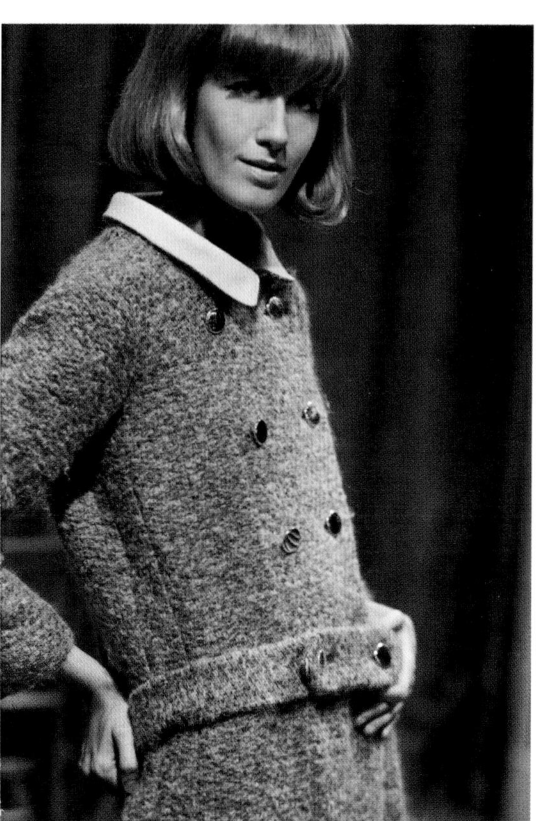

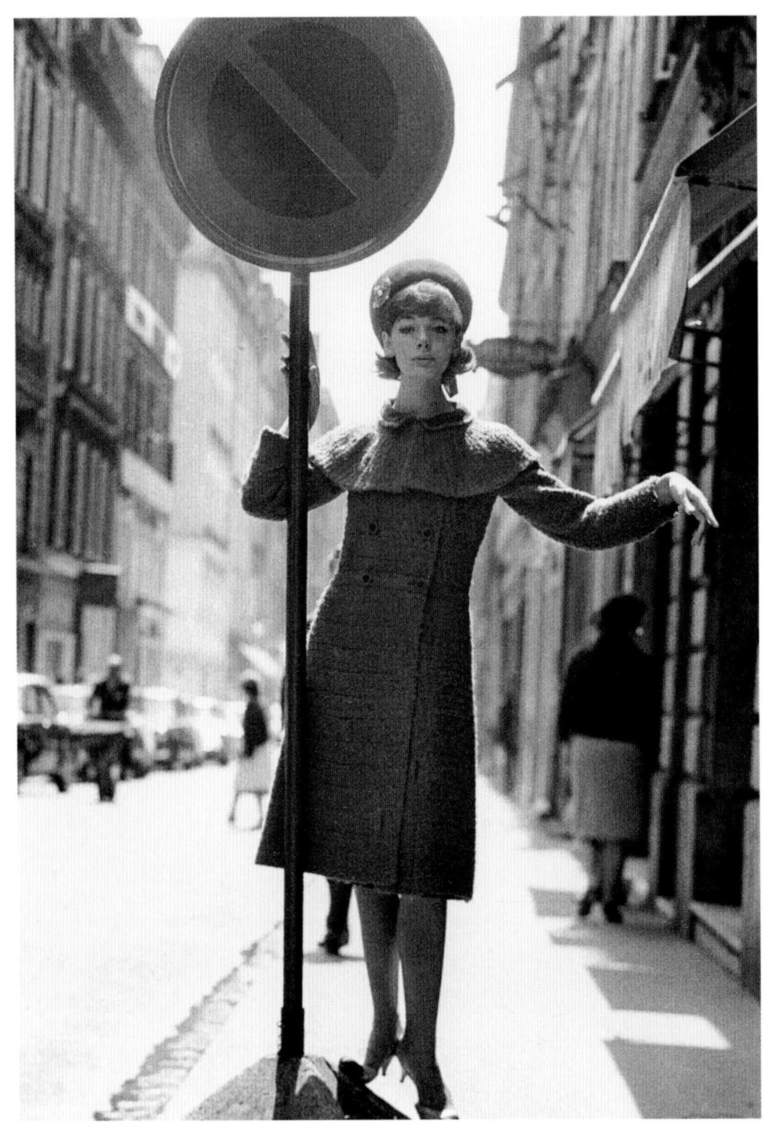

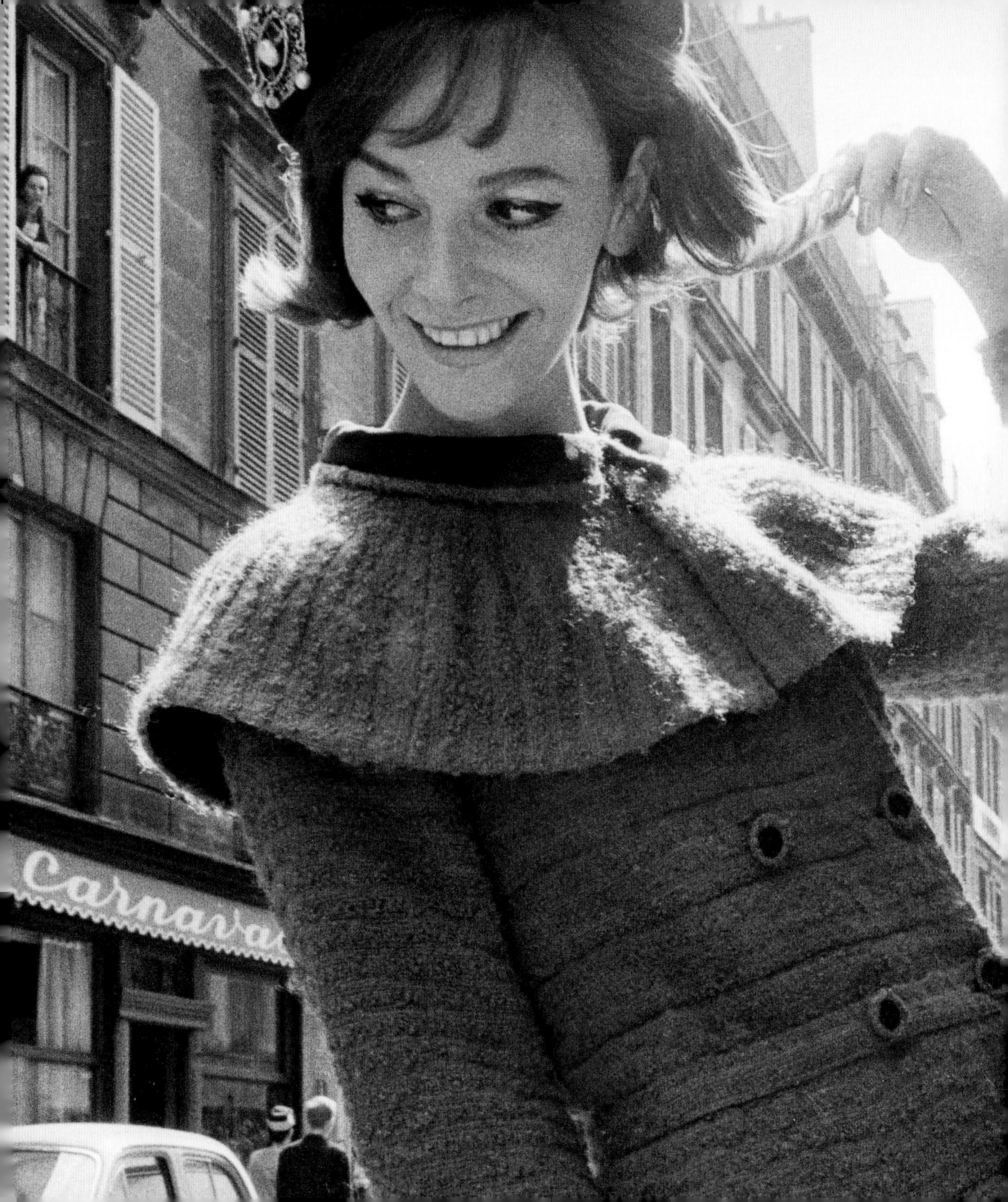
Carnava

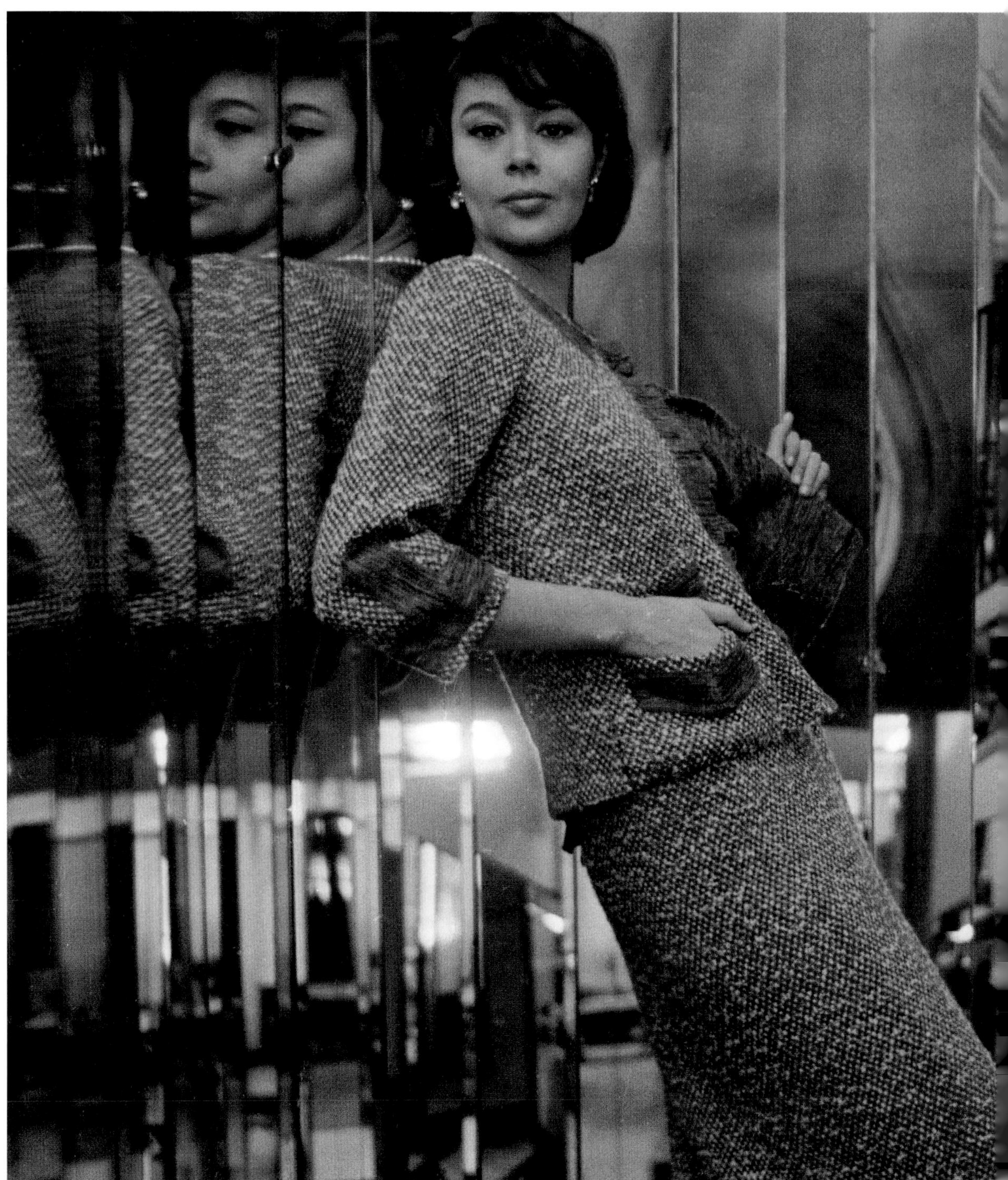

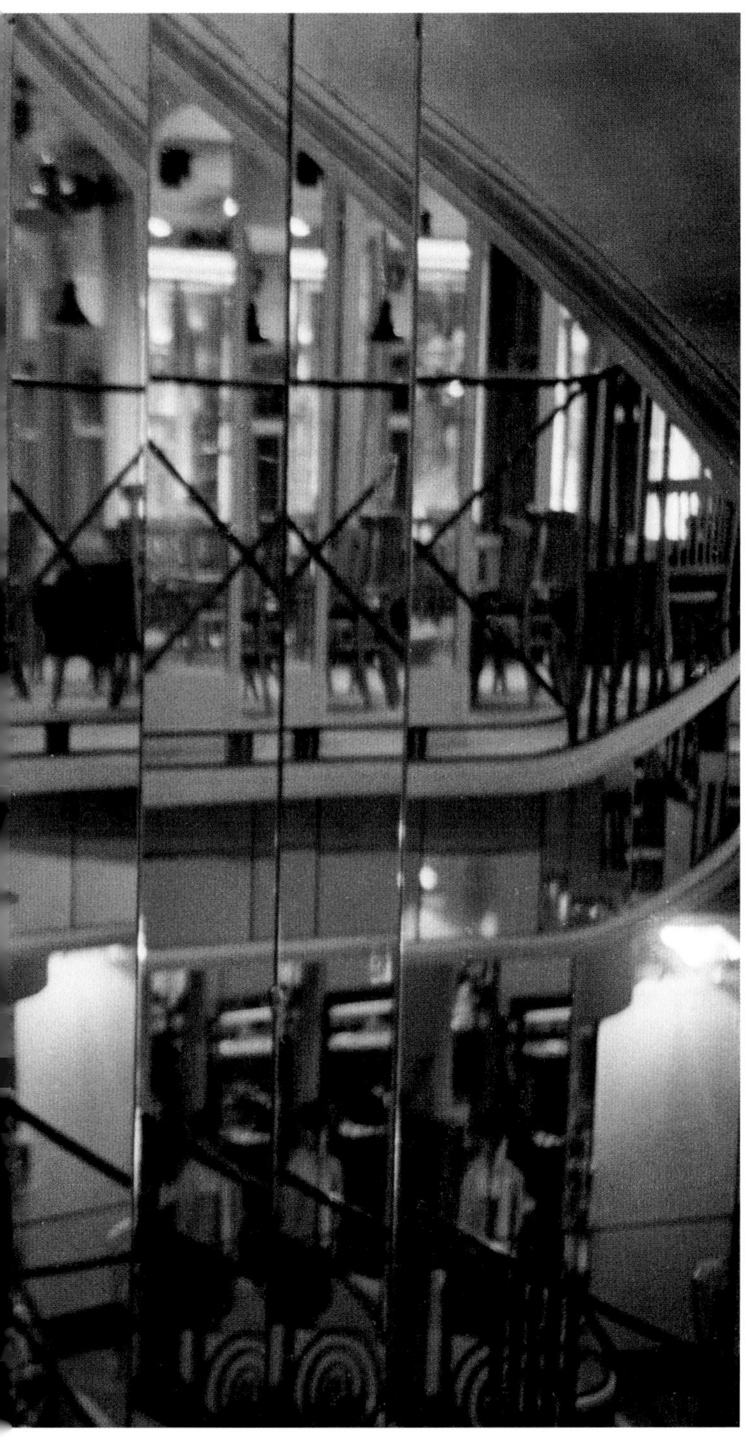

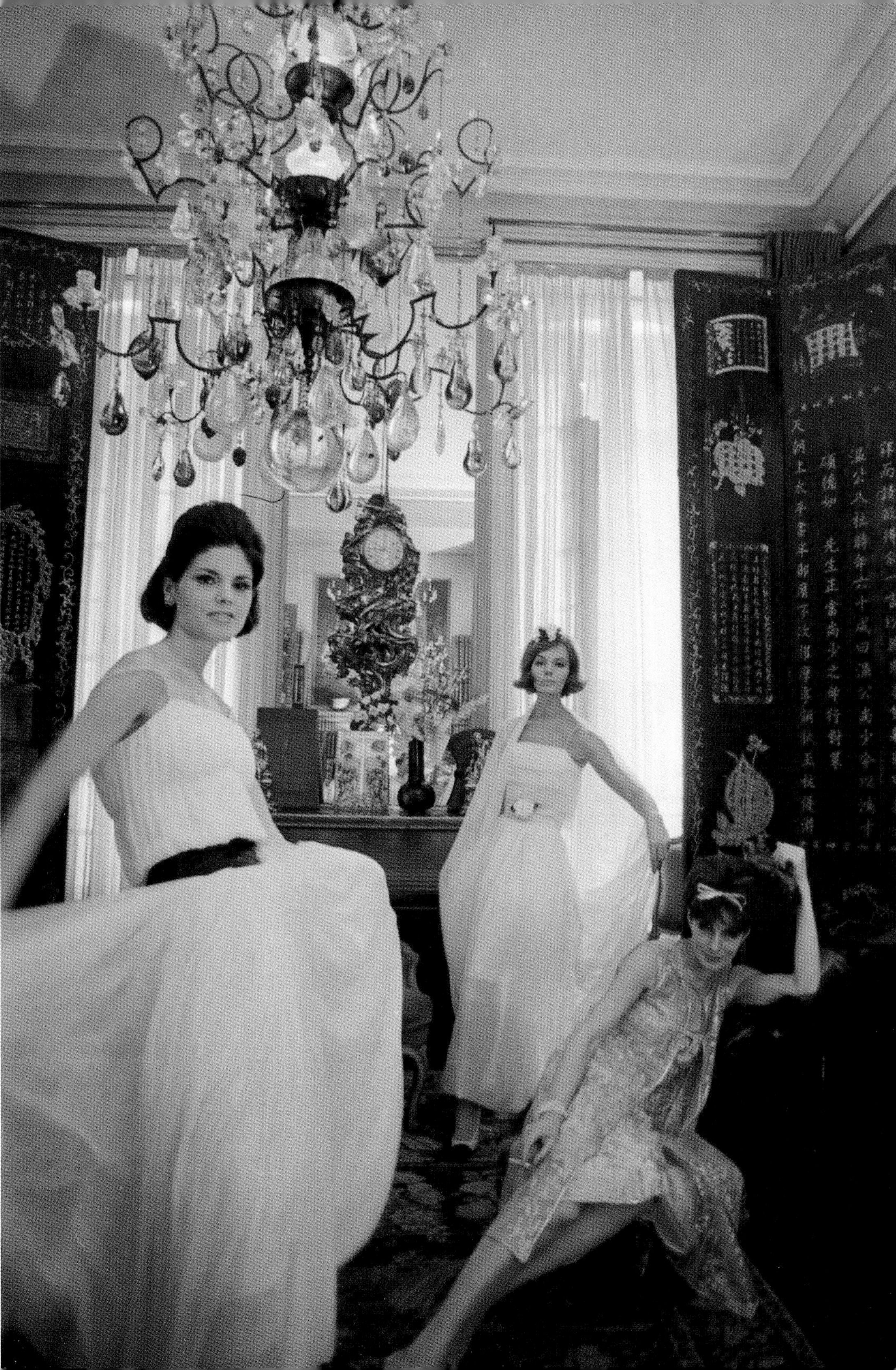

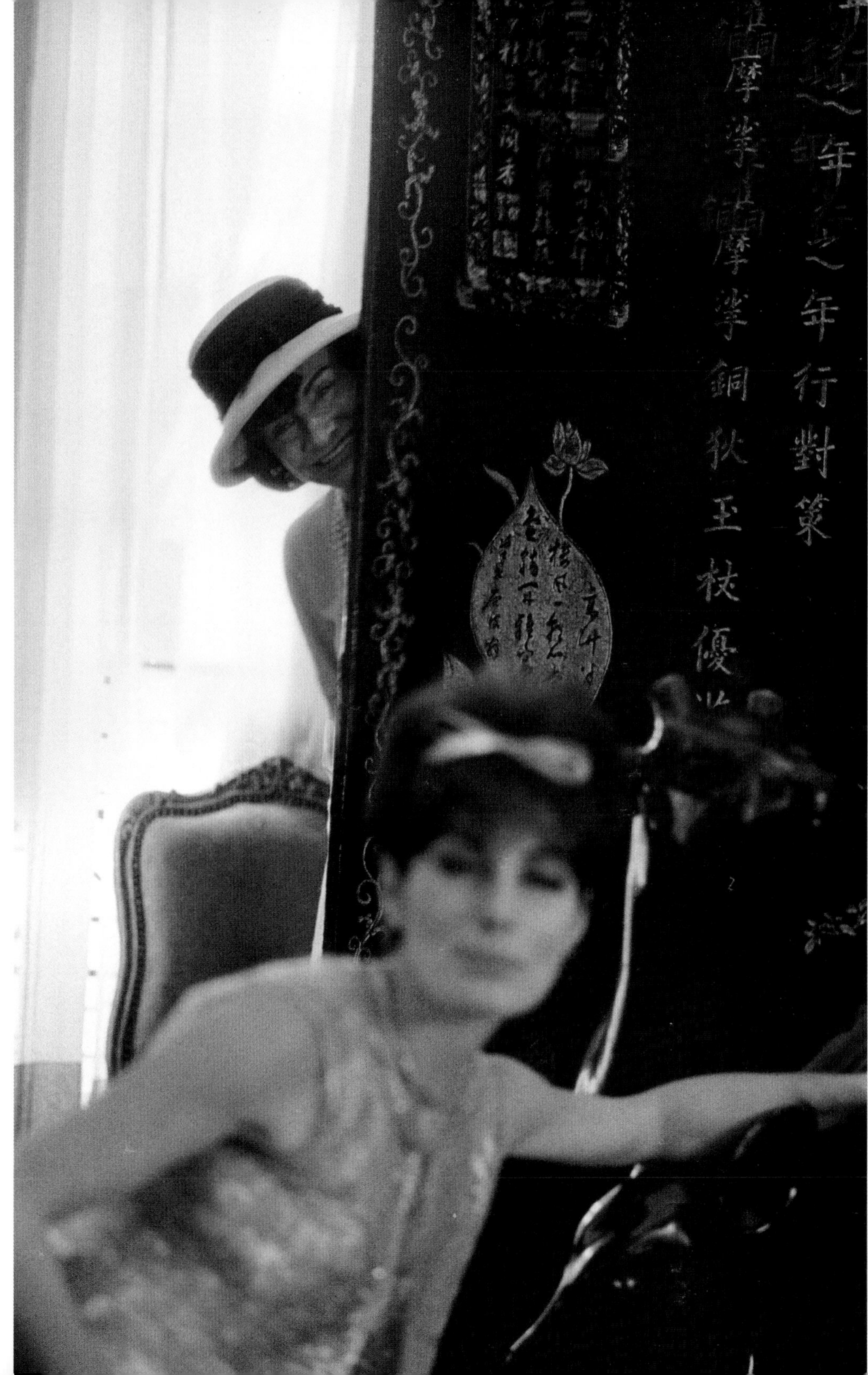

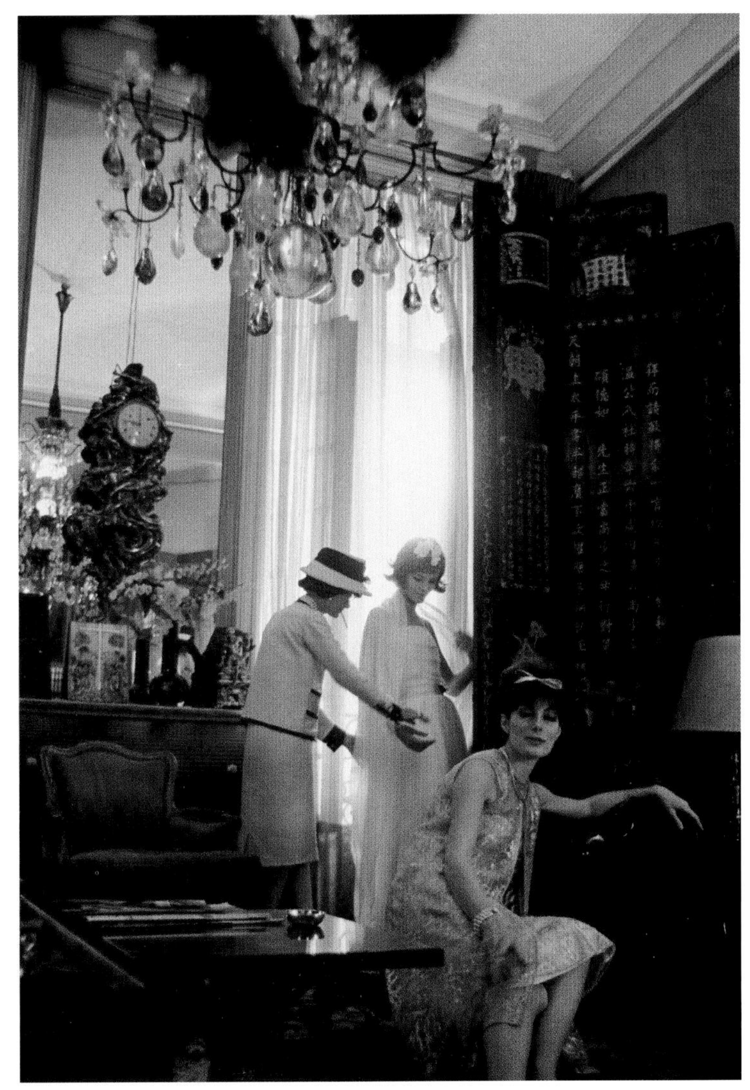

The first time Chanel acknowledged me and opened her world to me.

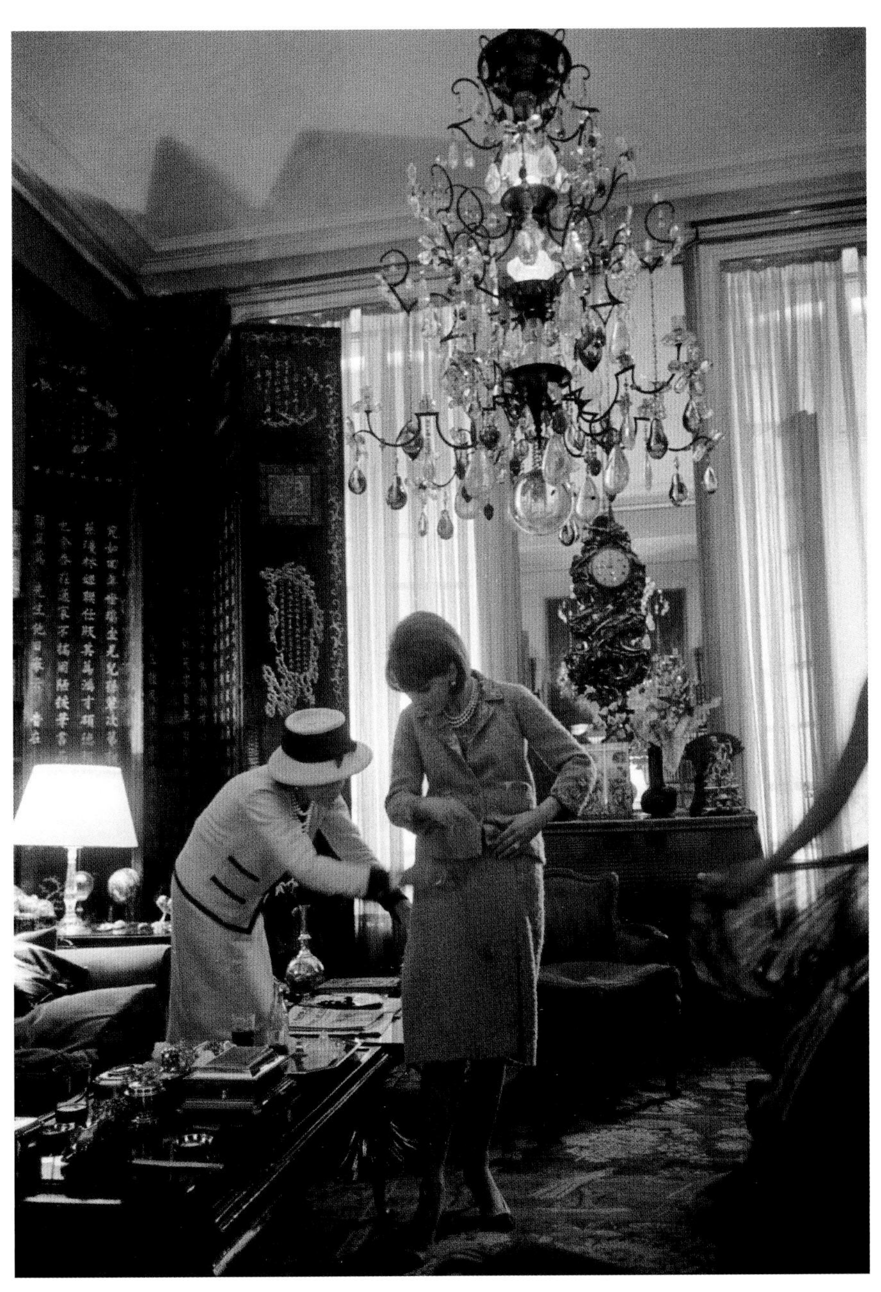

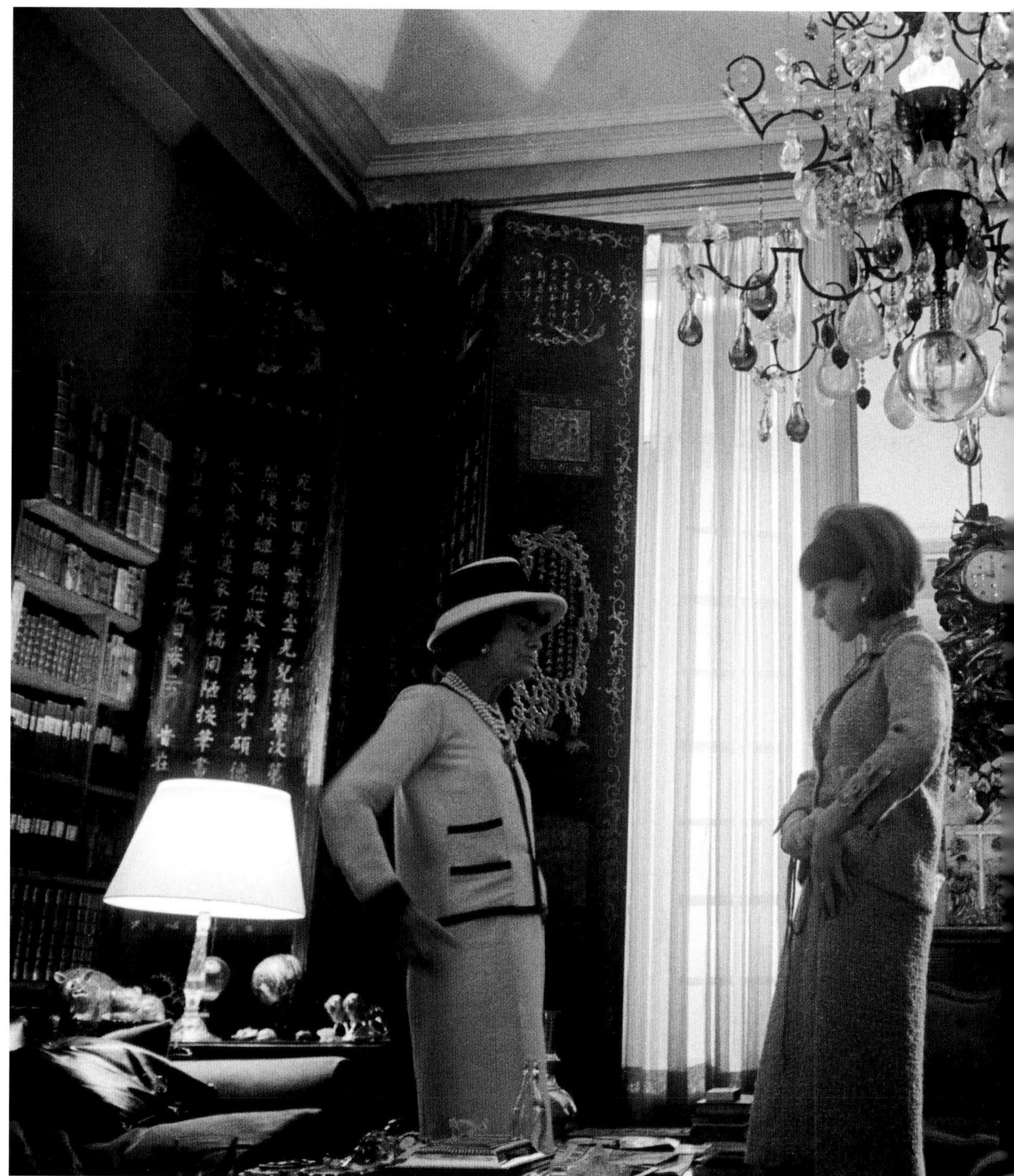

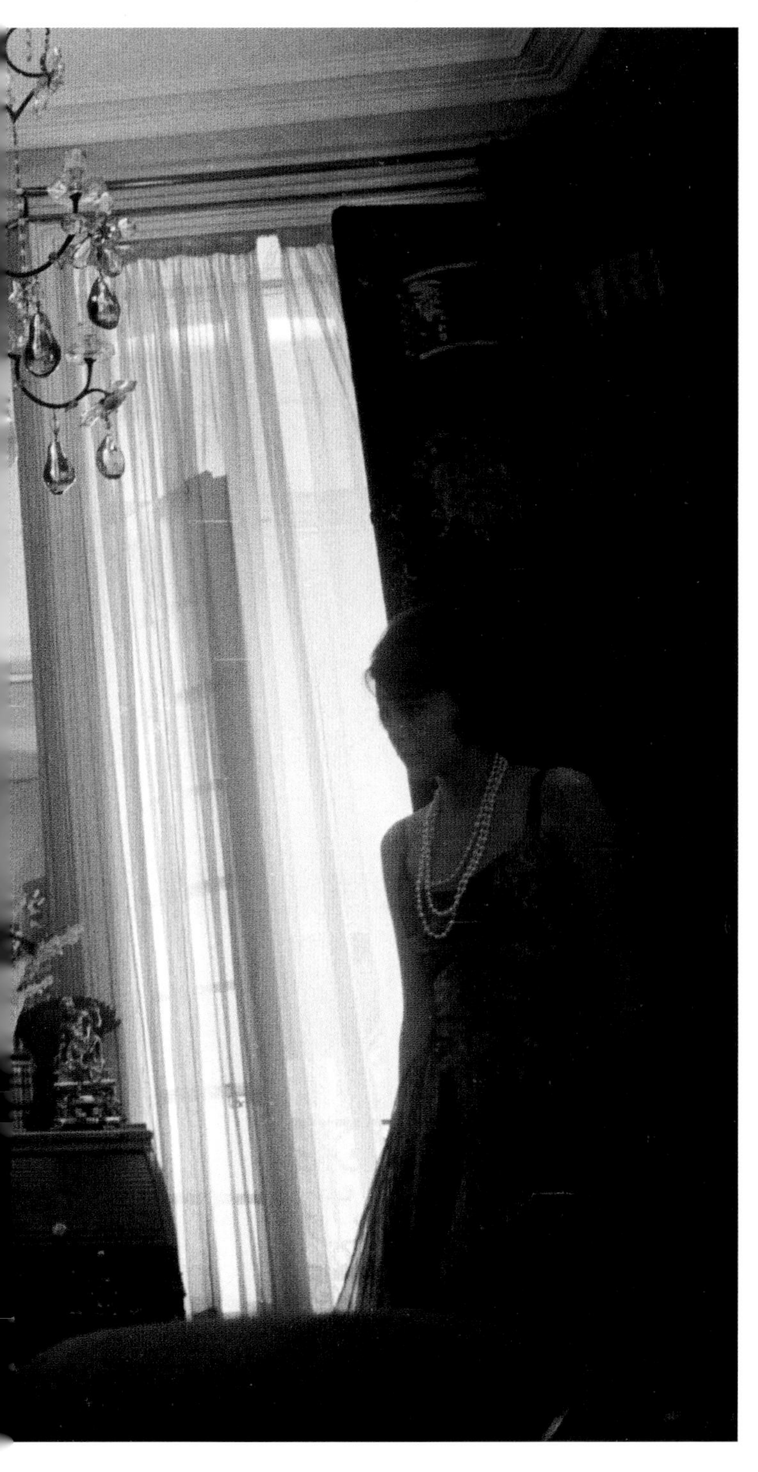

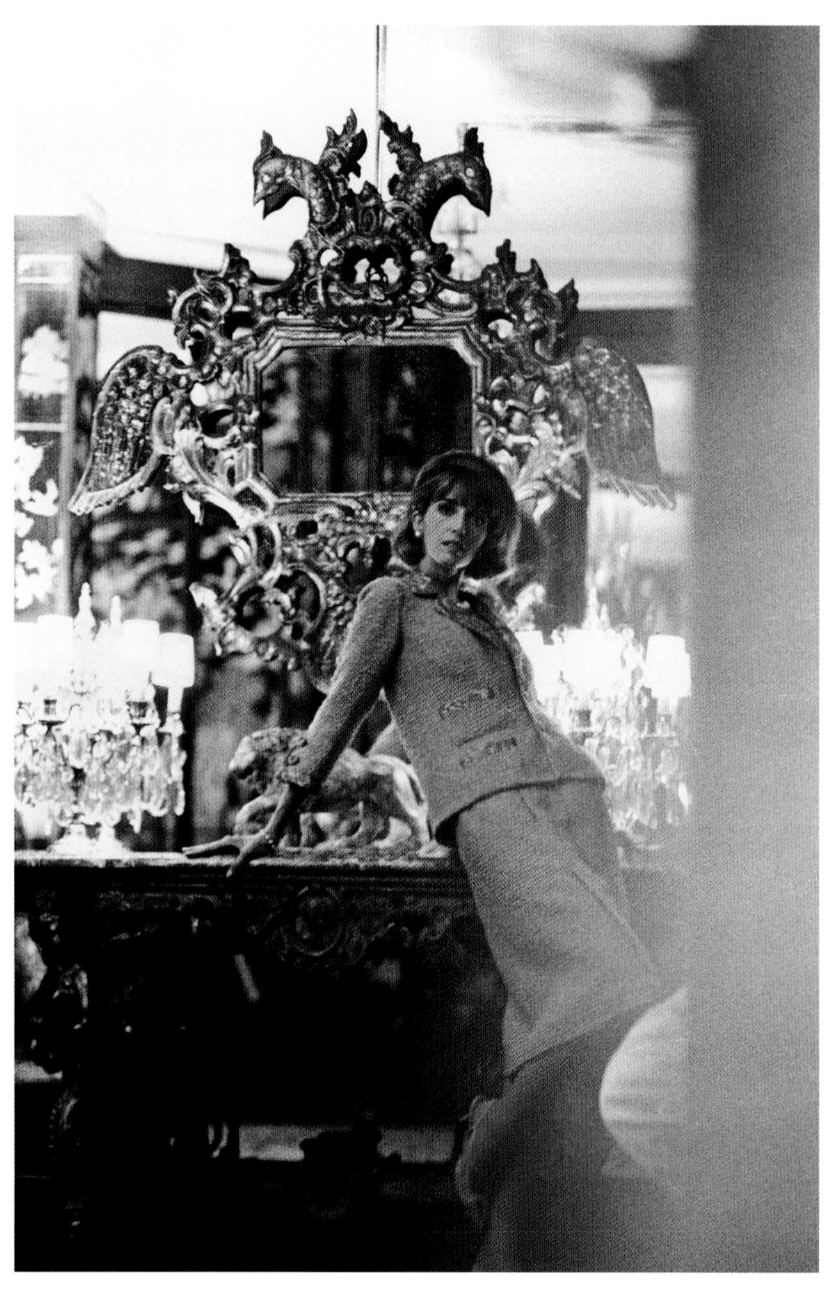

Jewelers widely copied Chanel's costume jewelry designs.

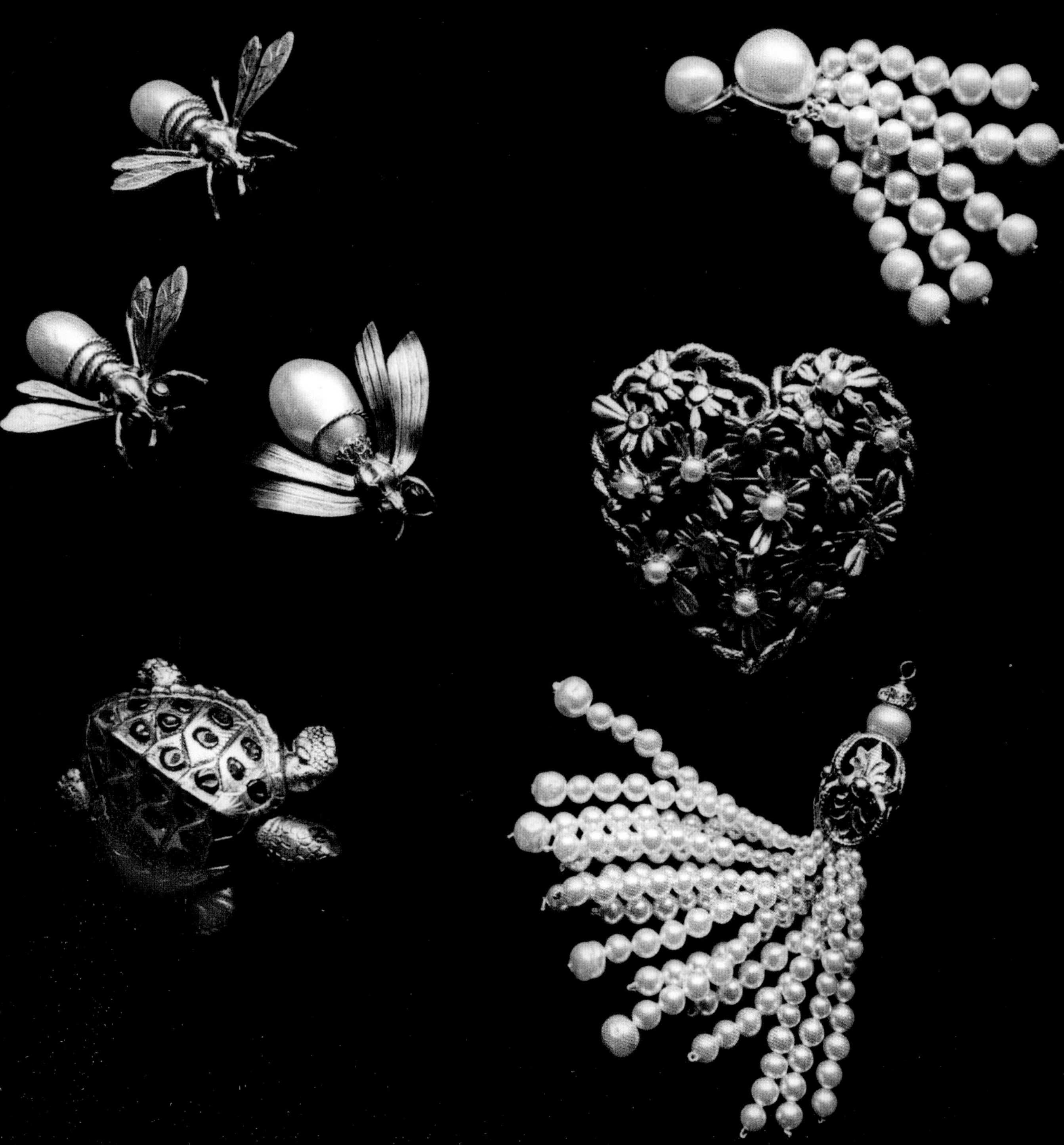

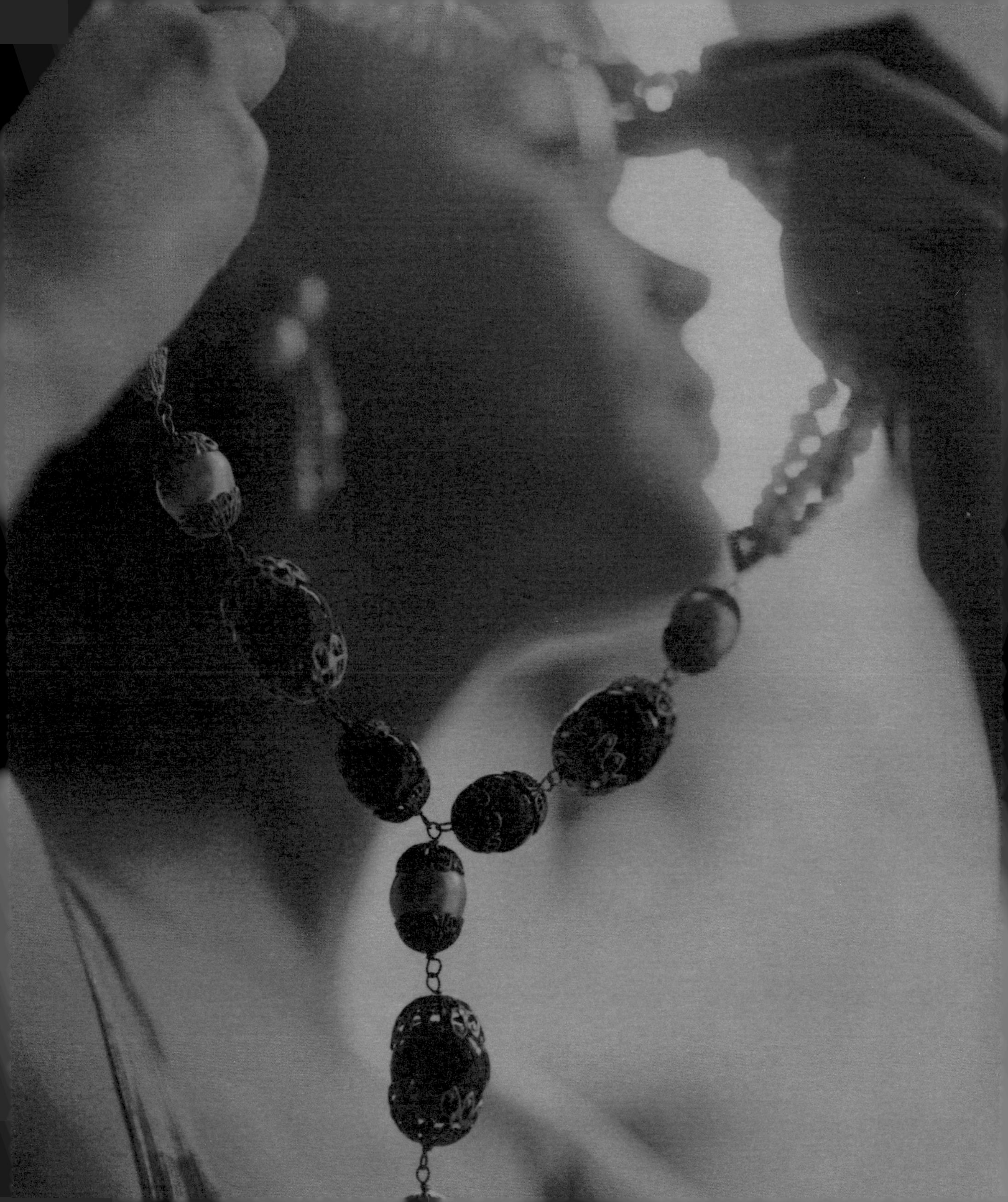

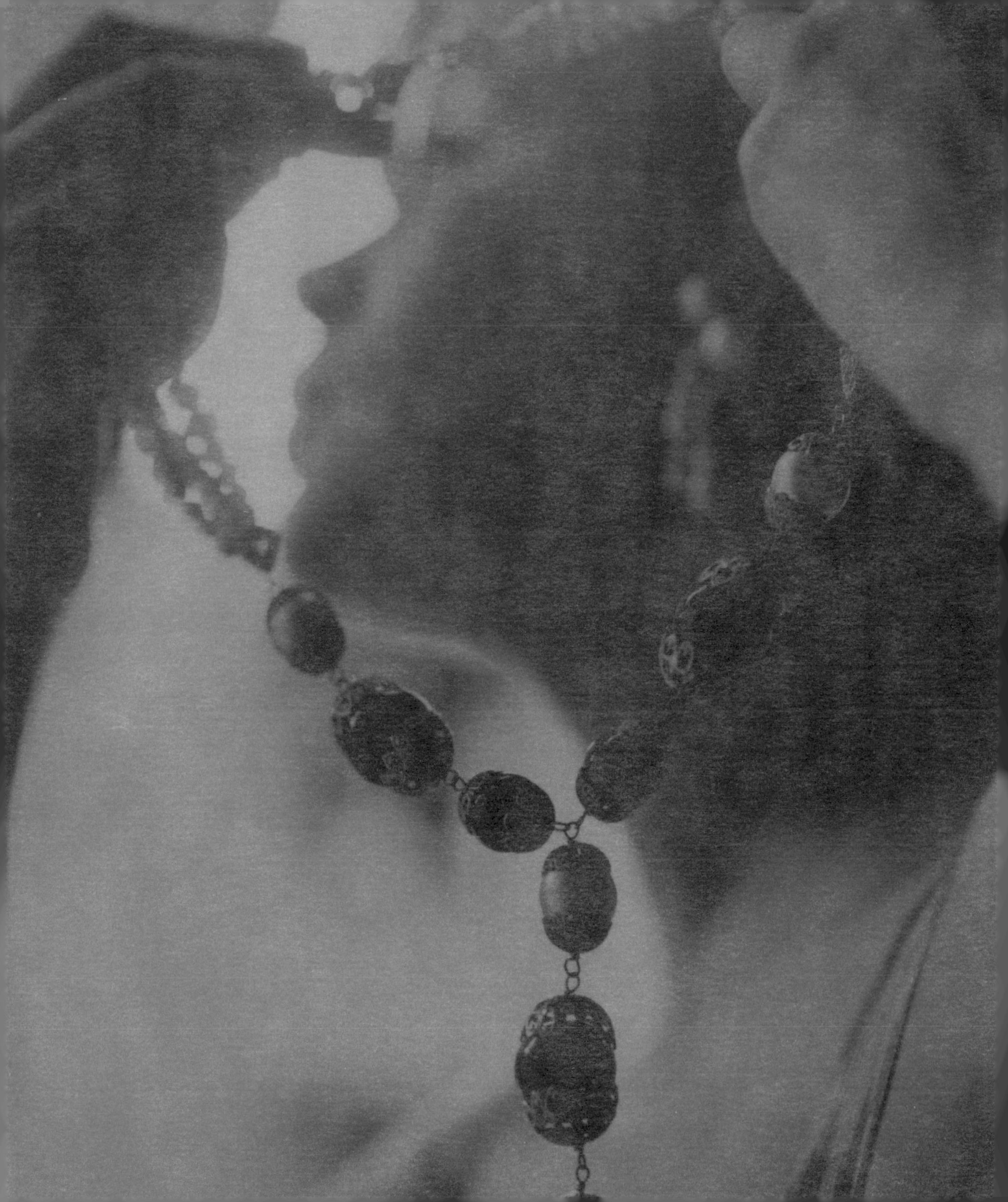

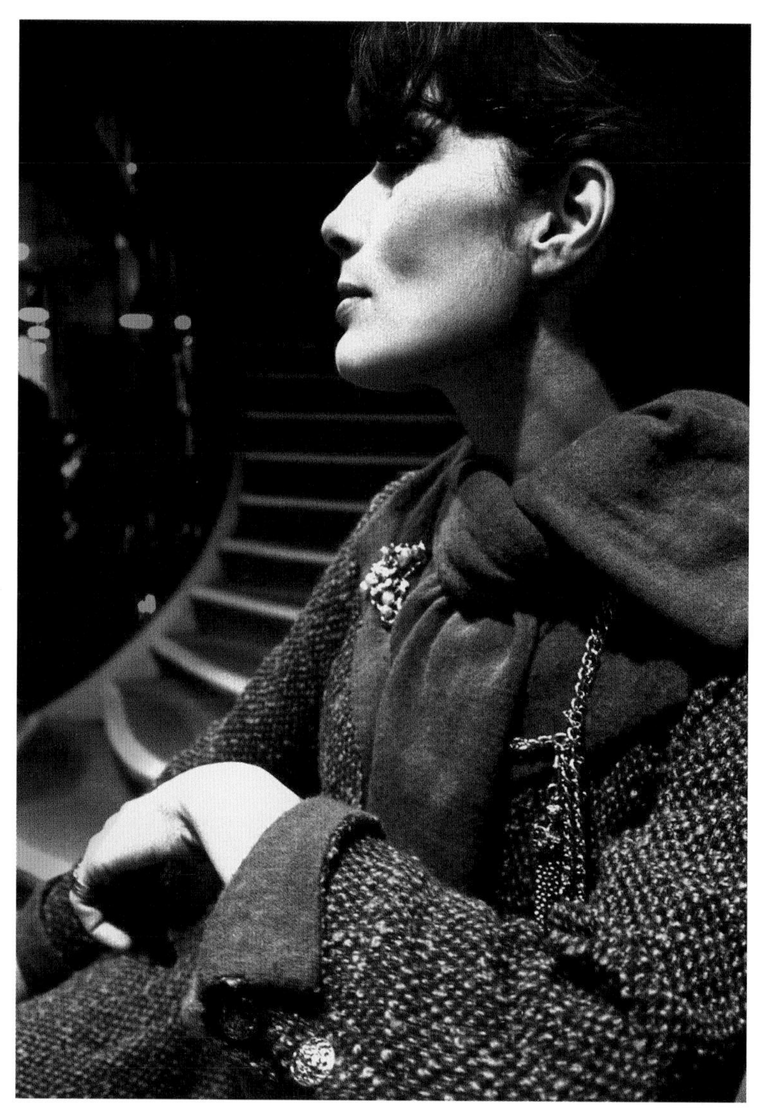

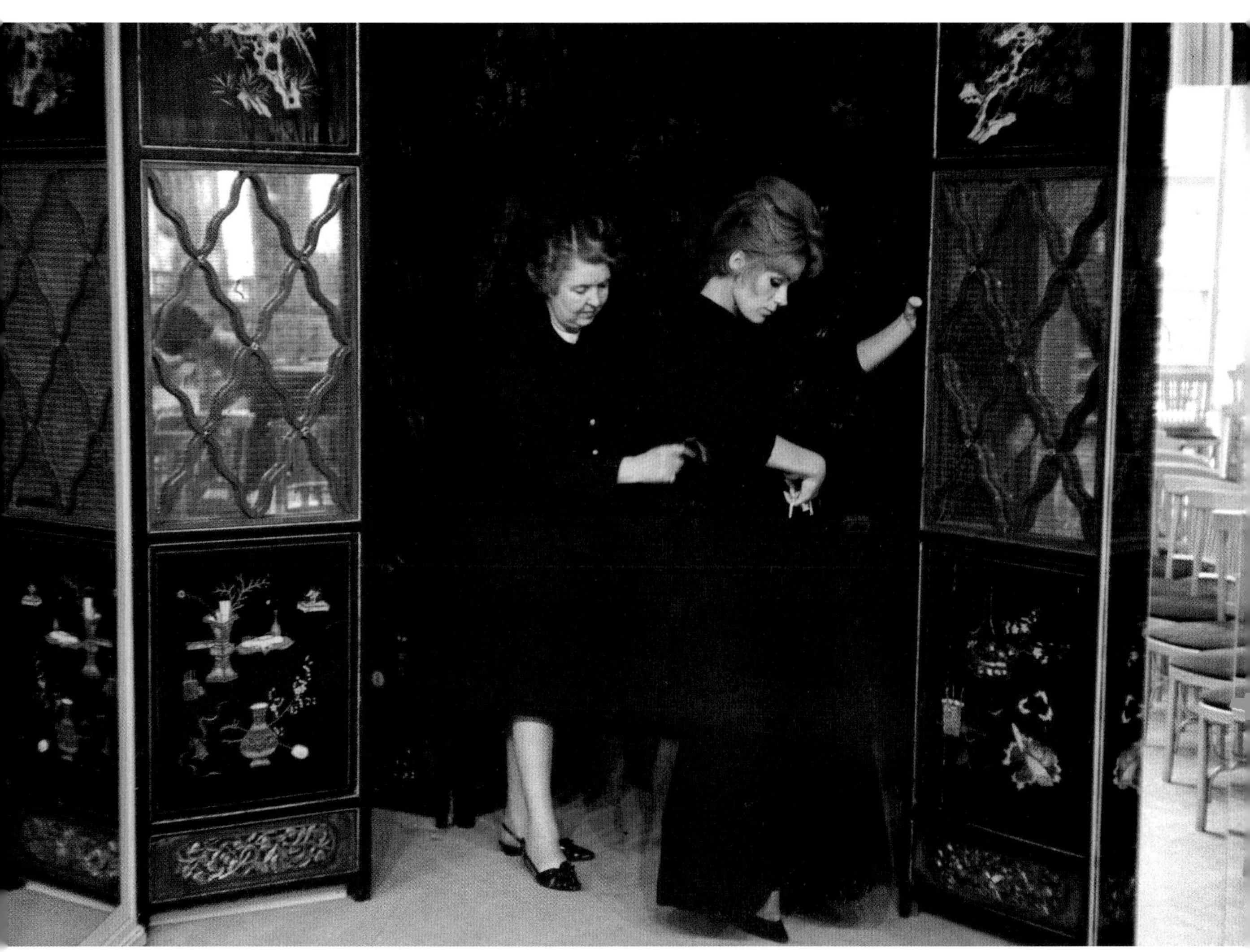

Actress Tammy Grimes being fitted in a couture gown.

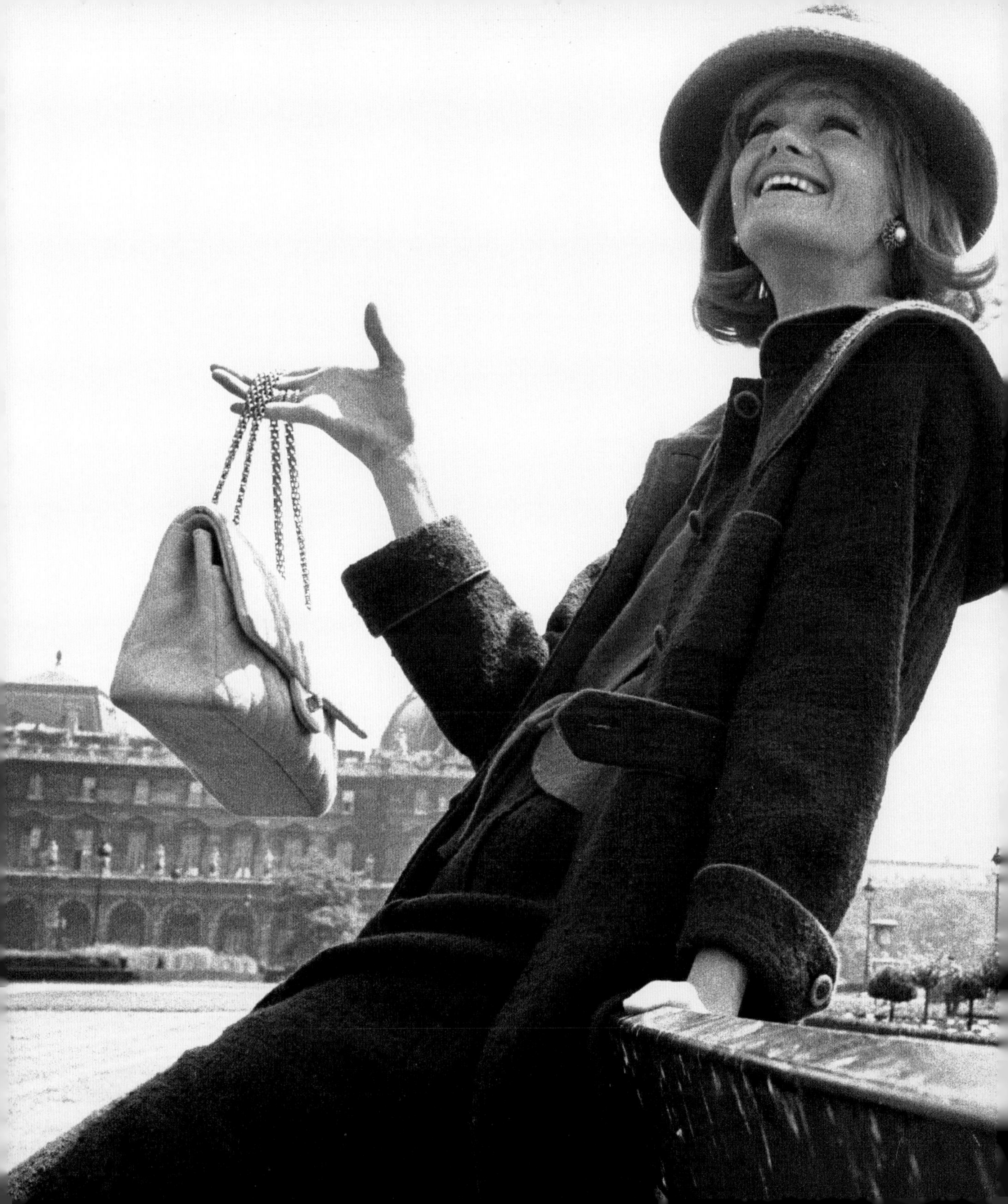

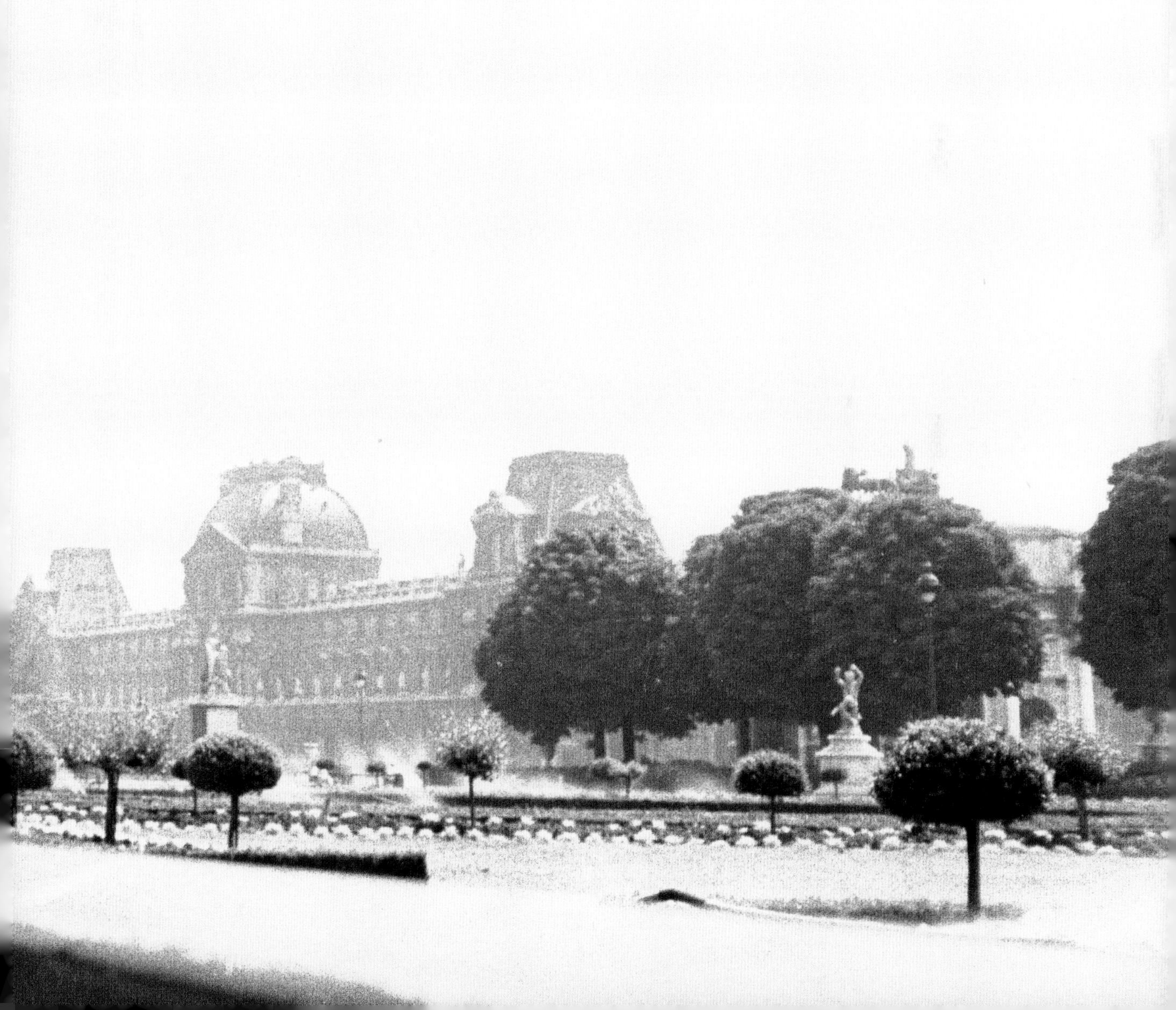

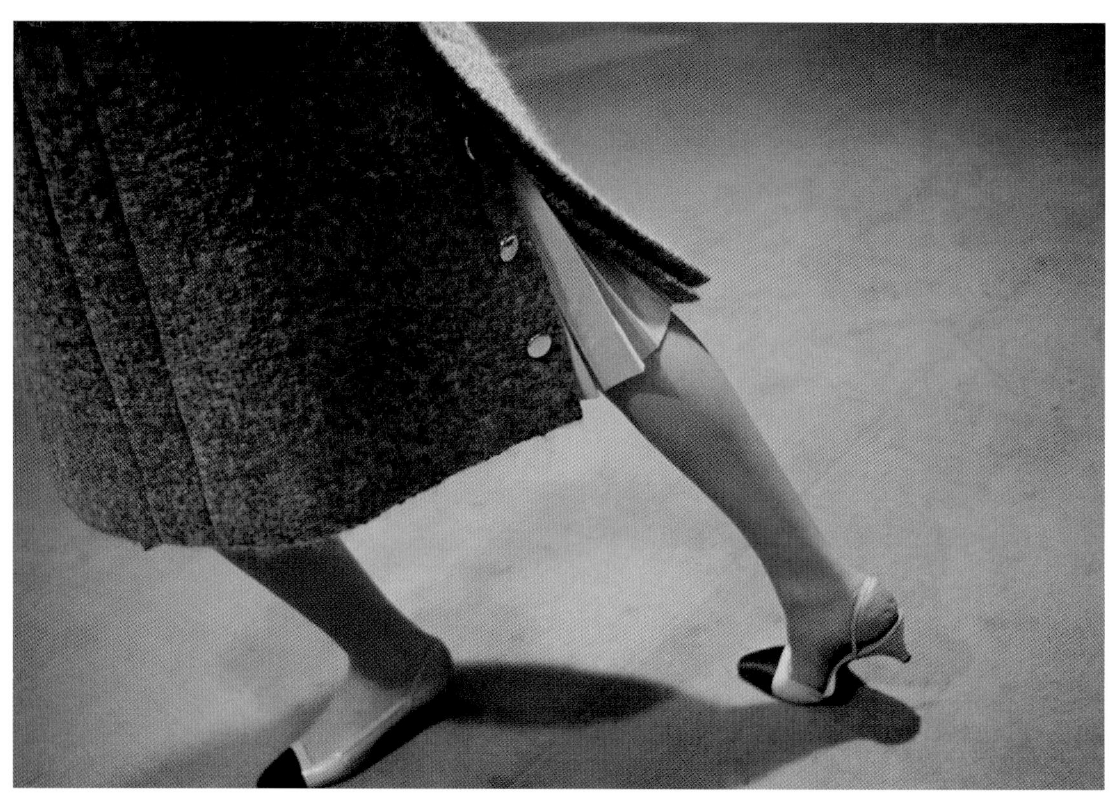

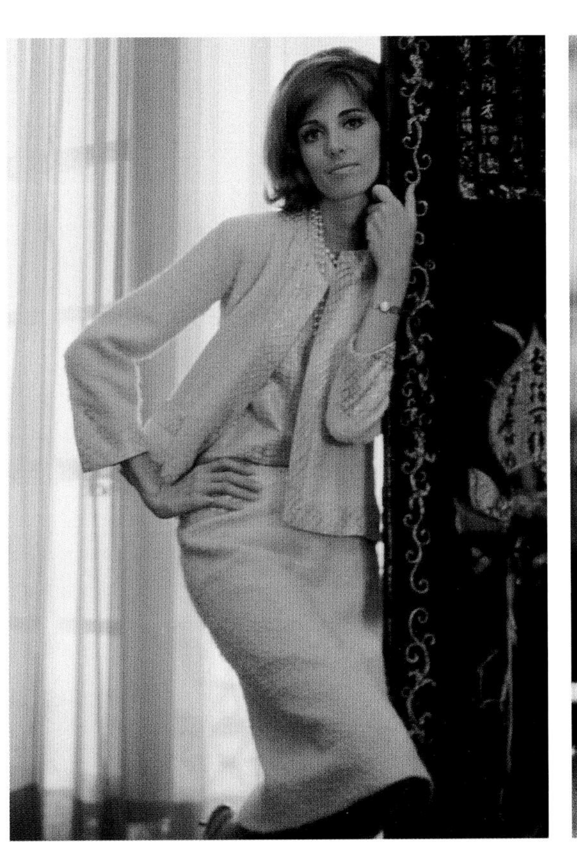

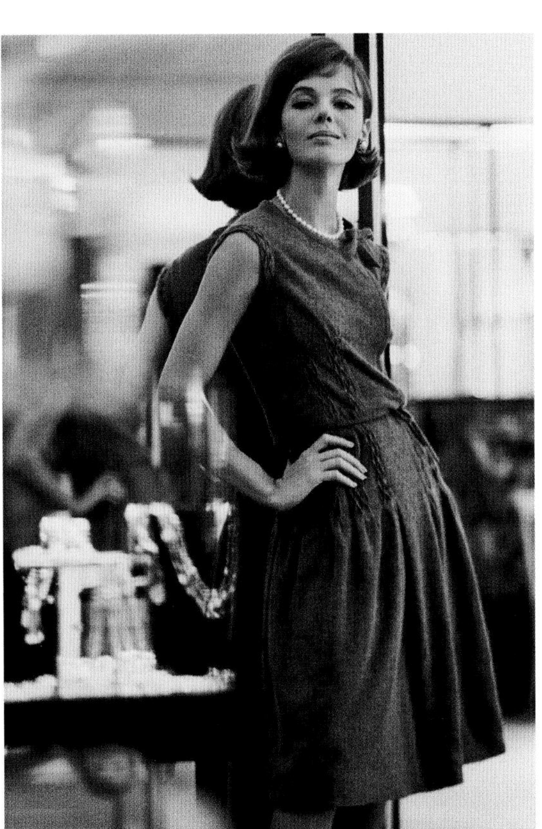

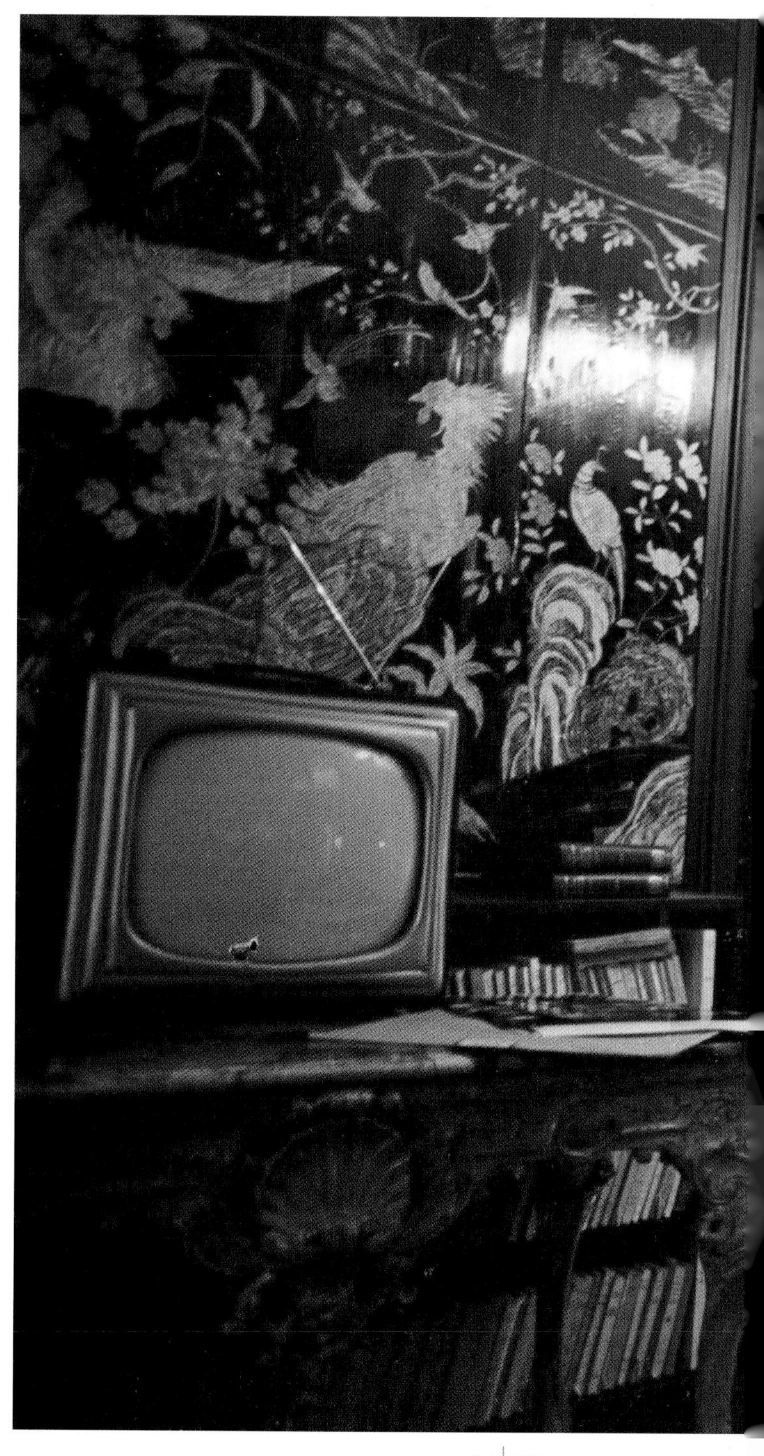

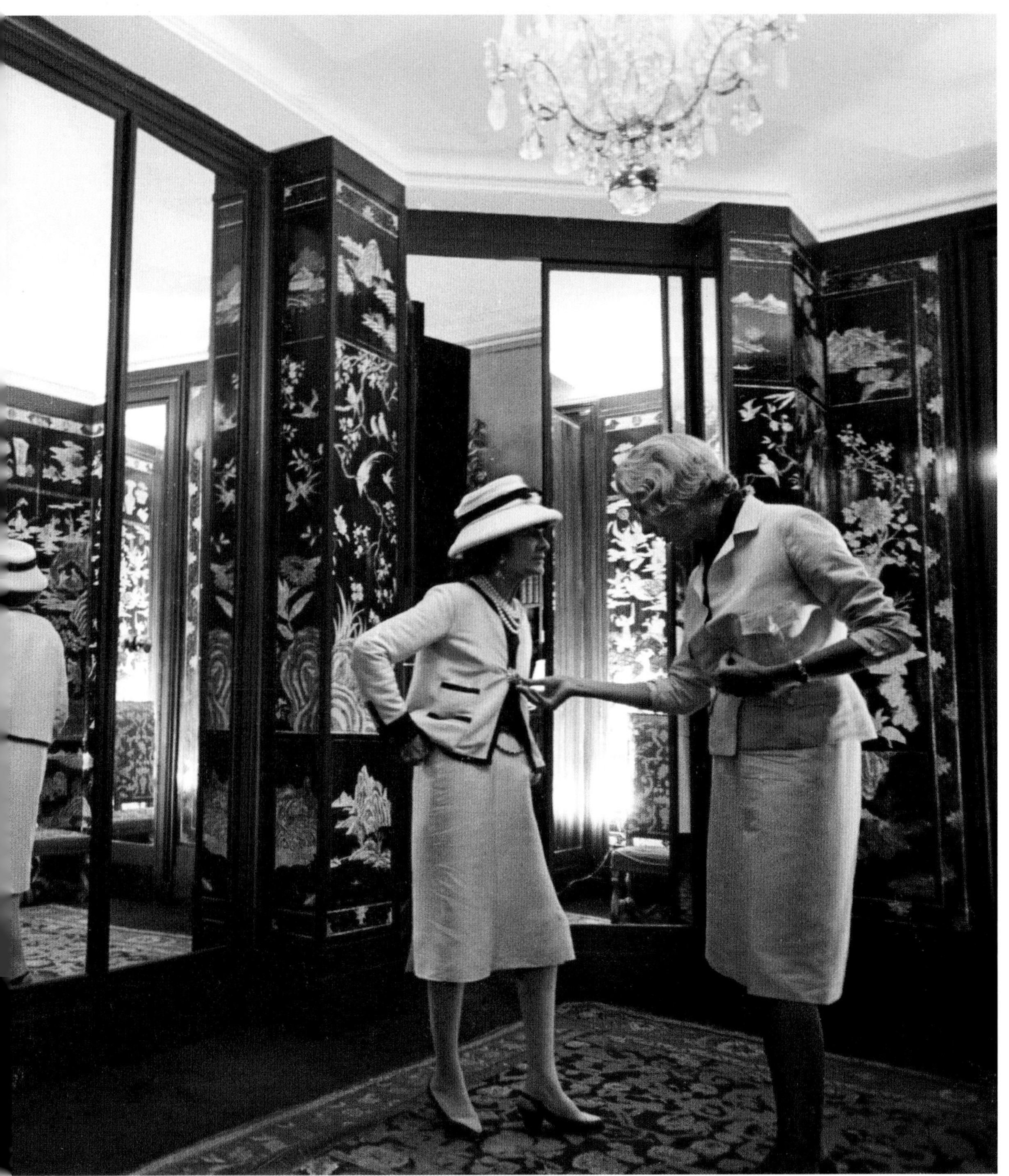

Chanel with client Claude Pompidou, who would become first lady of France in 1969.

There is no time for cut-and-dried monotony. There is time for work. And time for love. That leaves no other time.

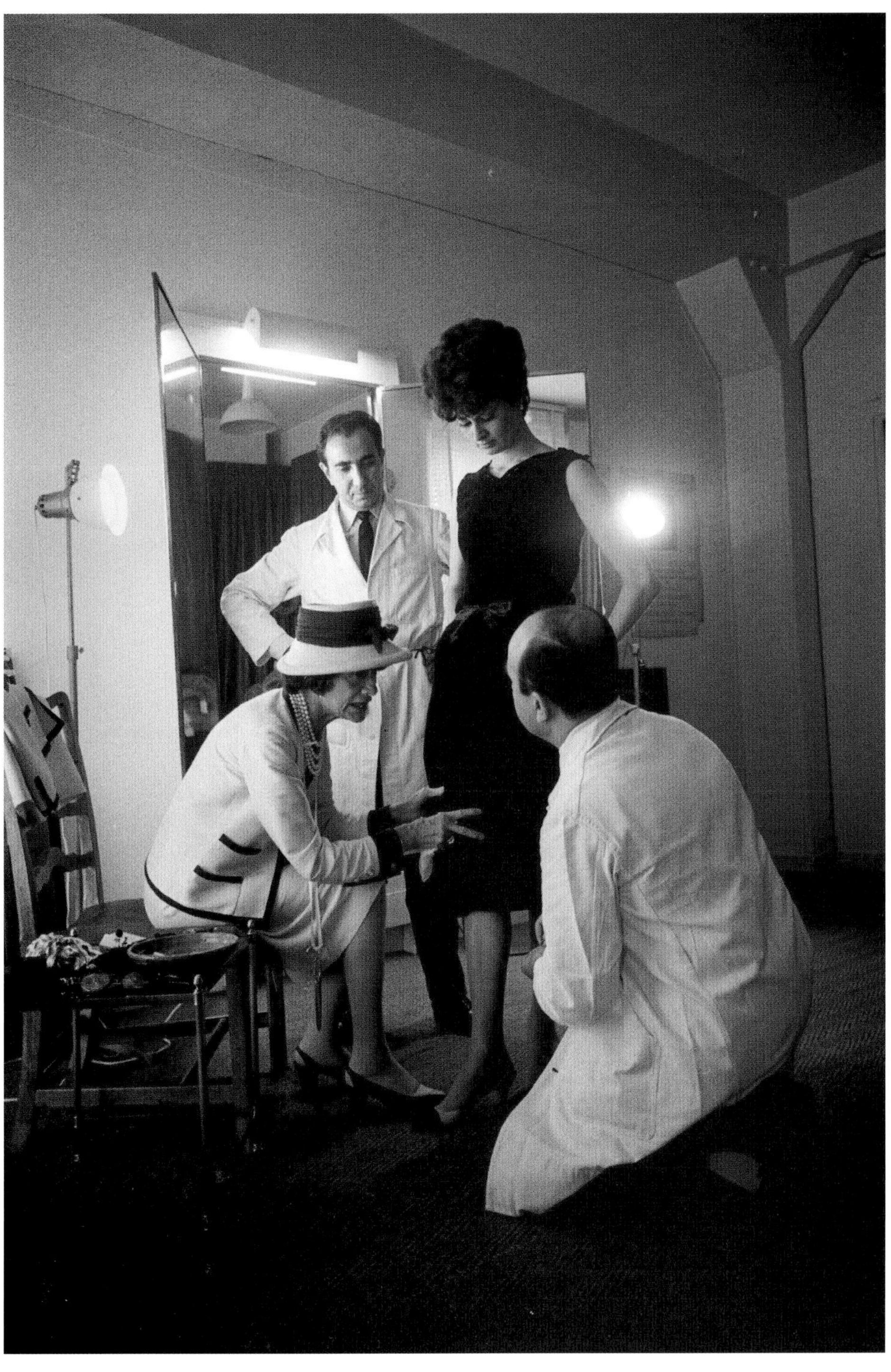

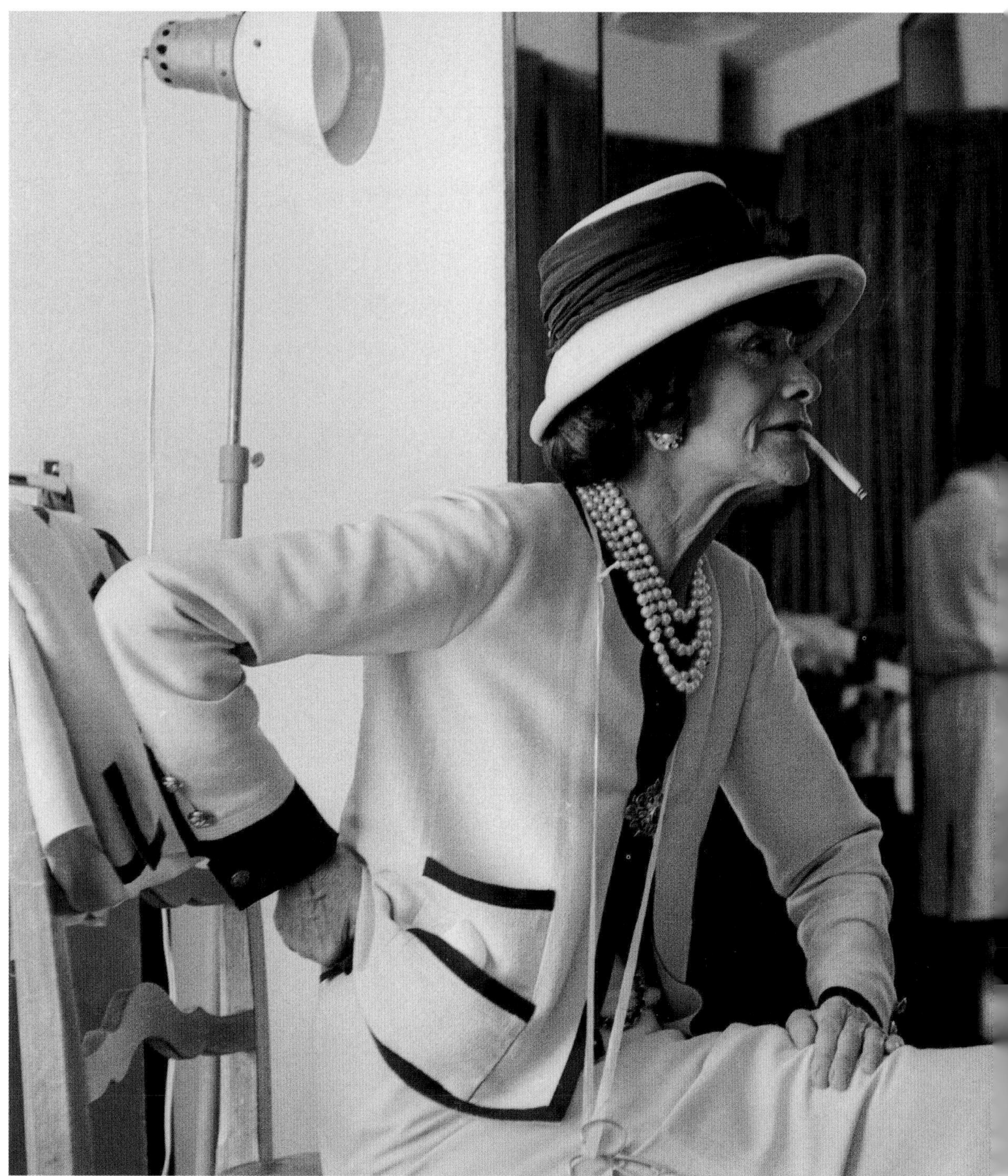

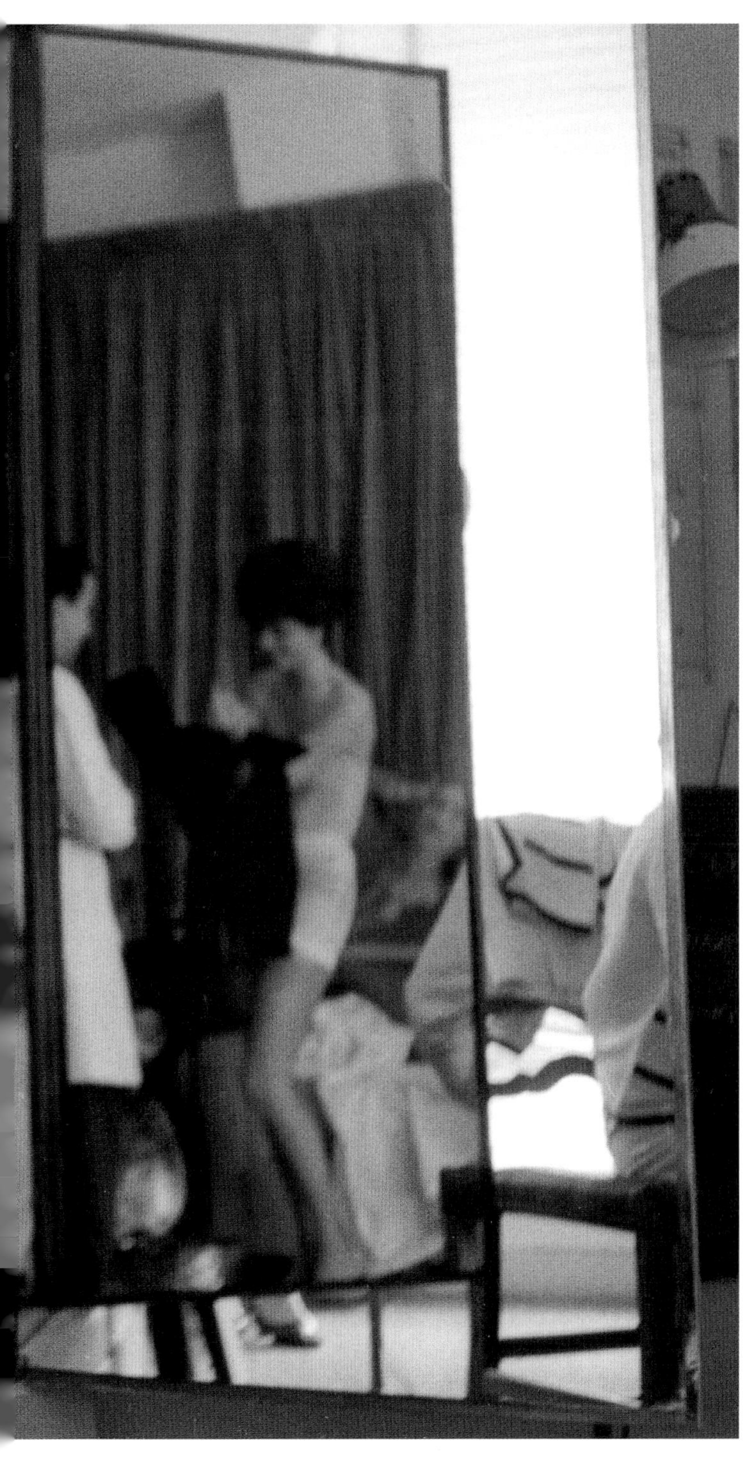

Mademoiselle at work, creating haute couture designs for the upcoming August collections.

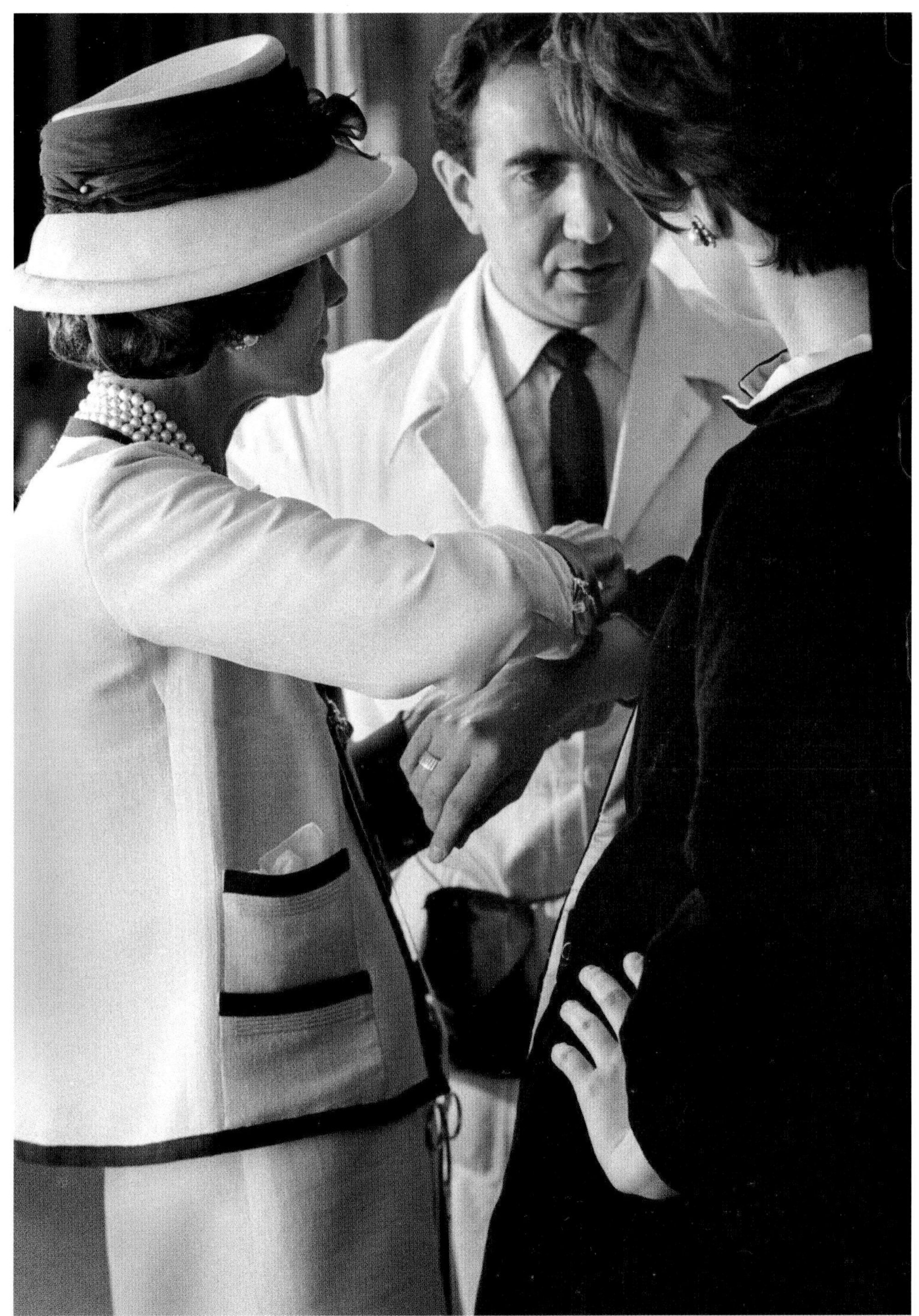

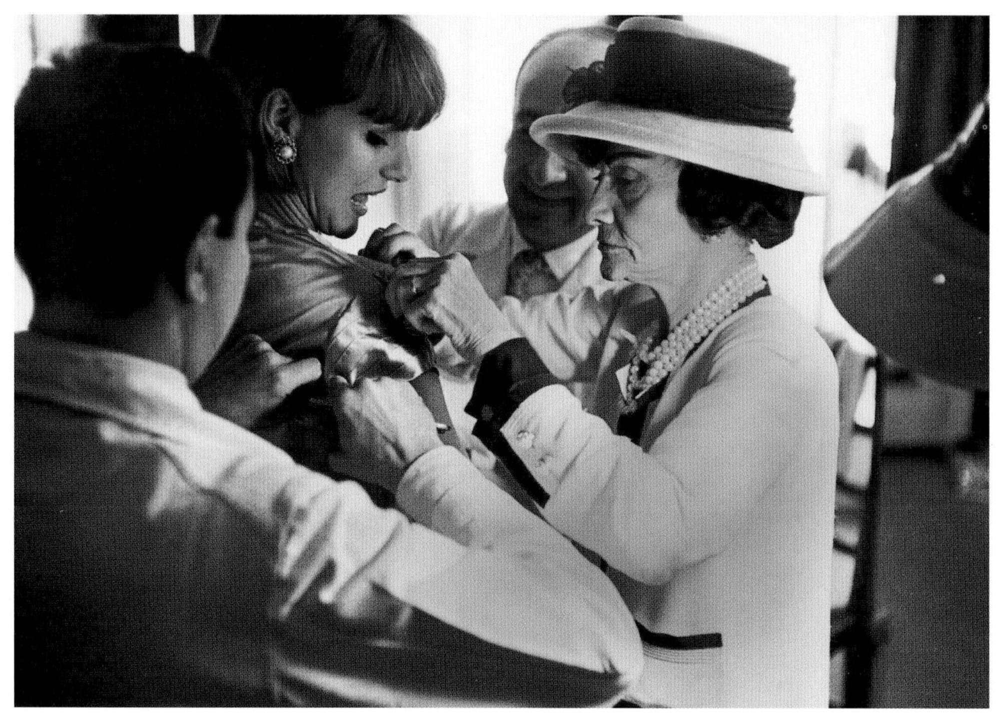

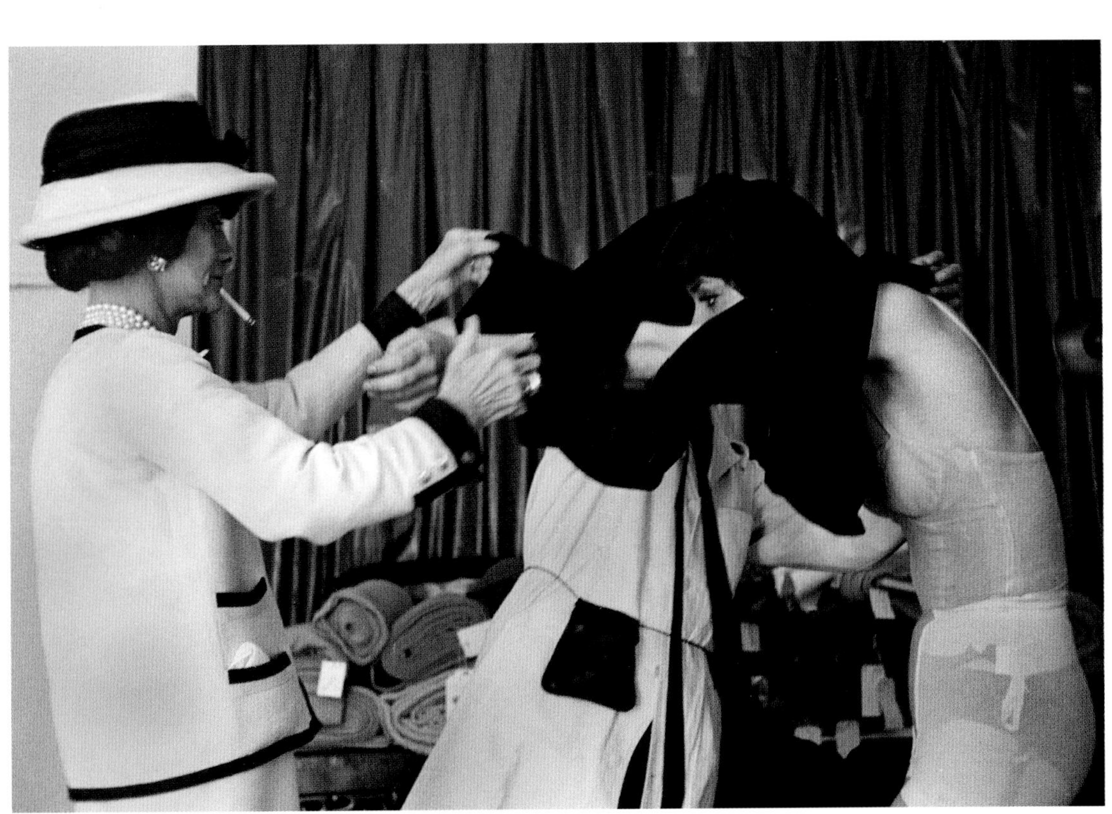

She lights her cigarettes with a 1925 Dunhill lighter, a gift. "I prefer to keep mementos rather than photographs."

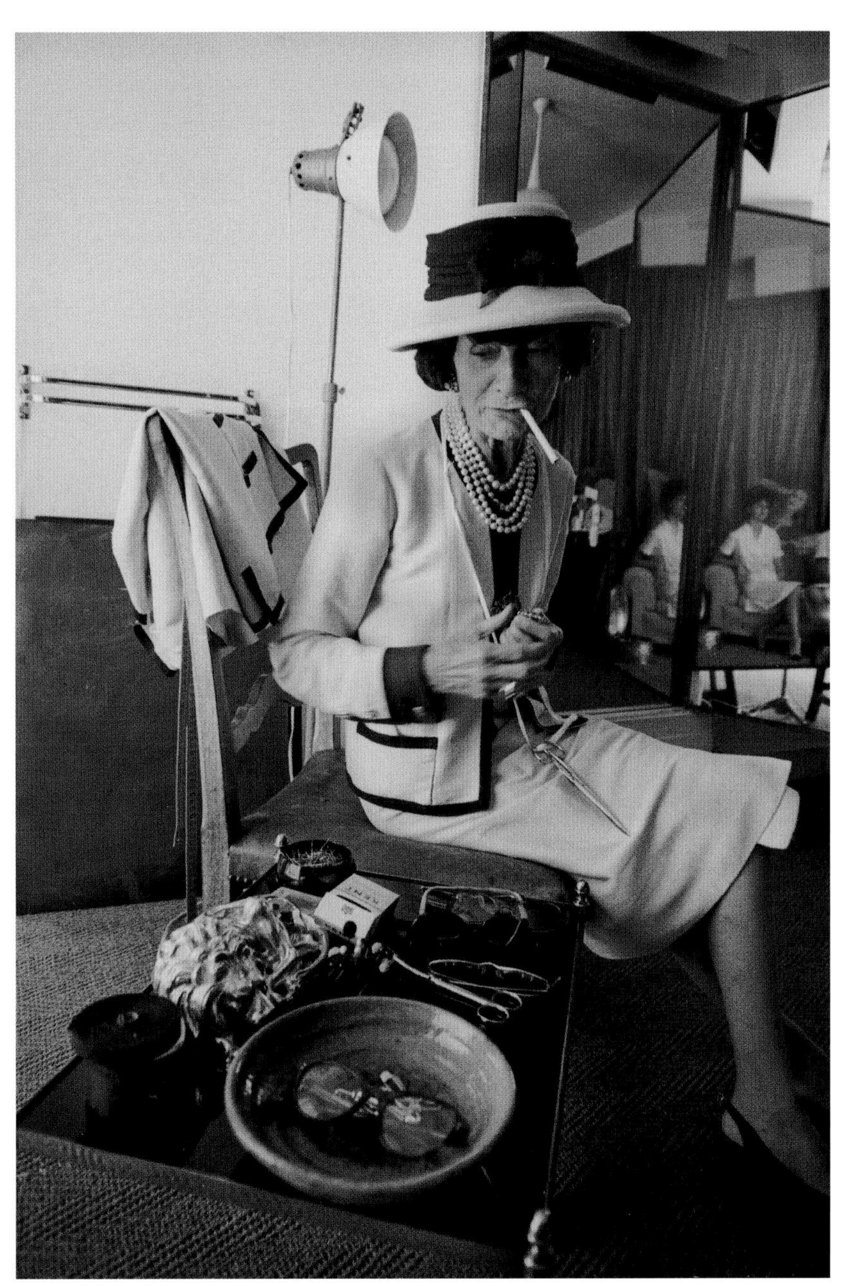

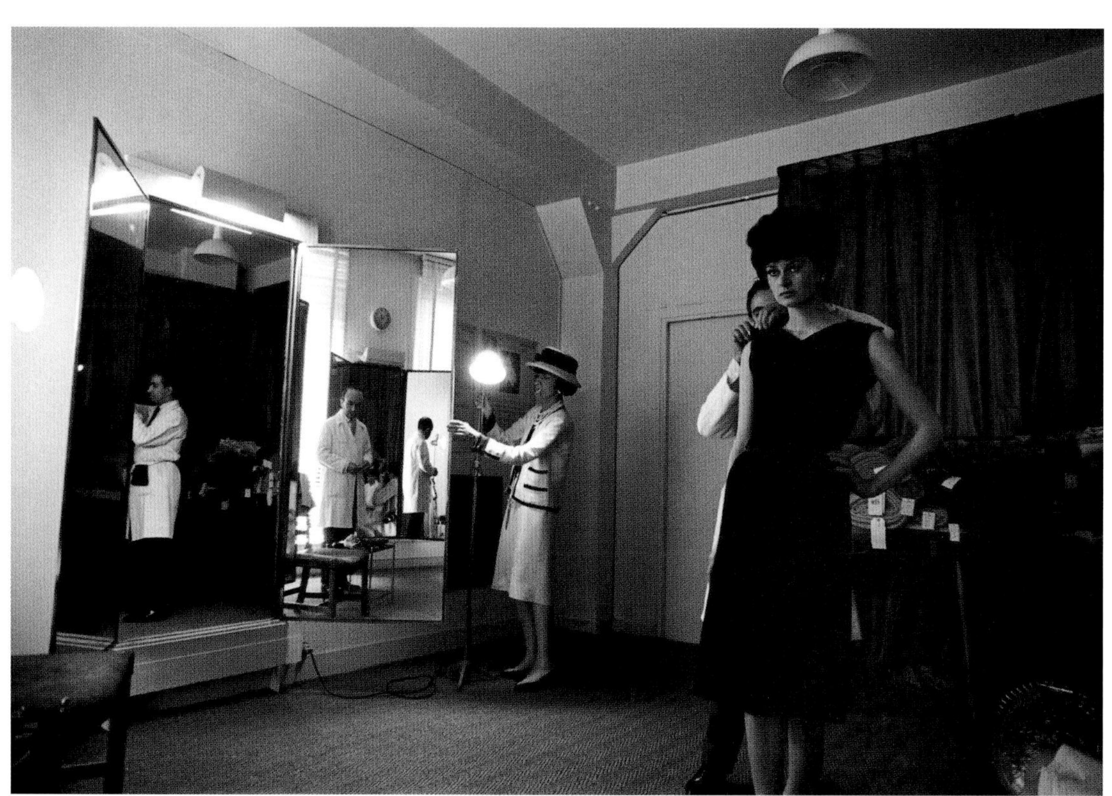

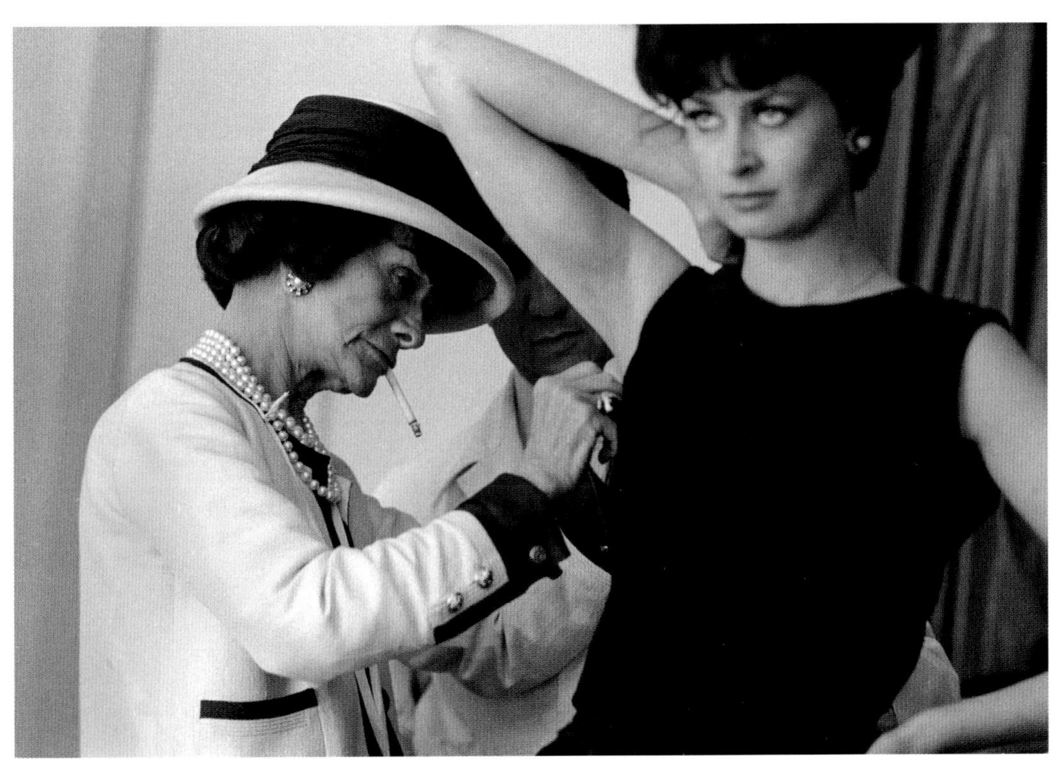

Chanel always strived for perfection. "I sculpt what I design."

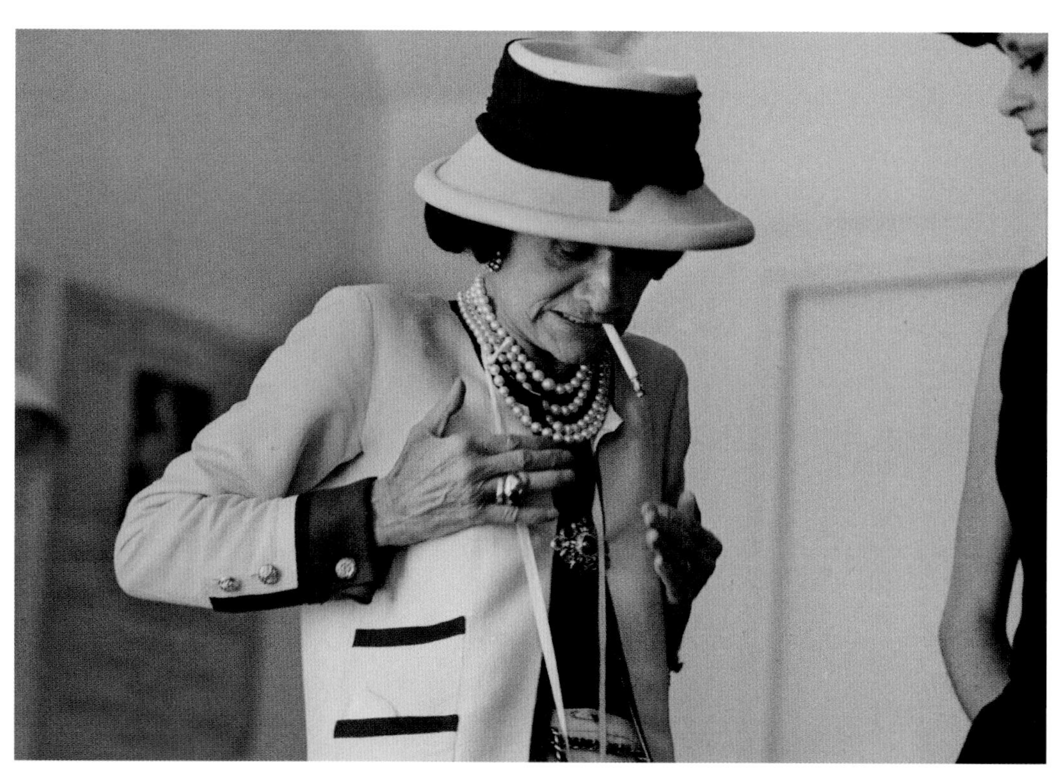

"I design for the bustline. I want to see the girl underneath the fabric."

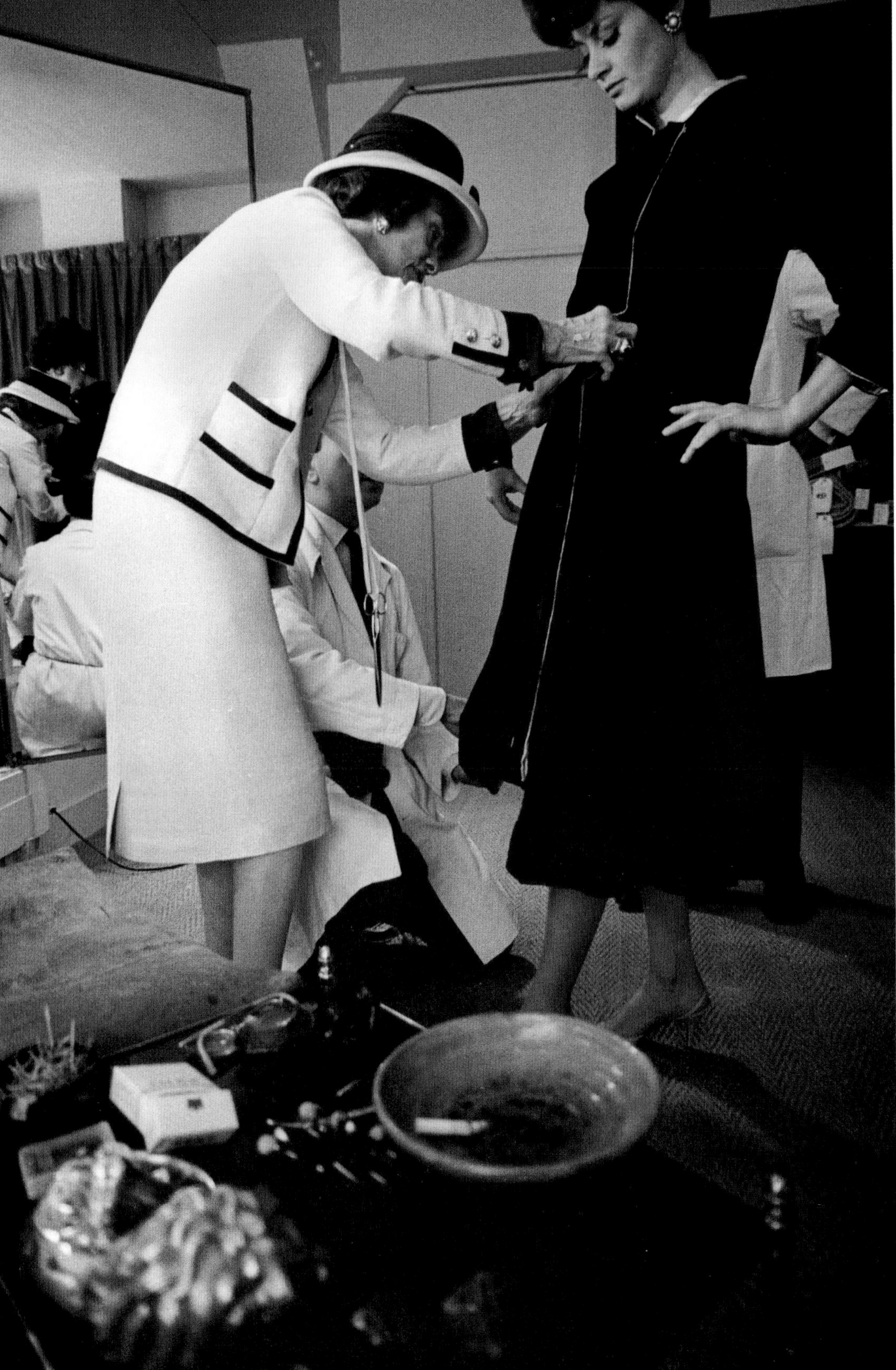

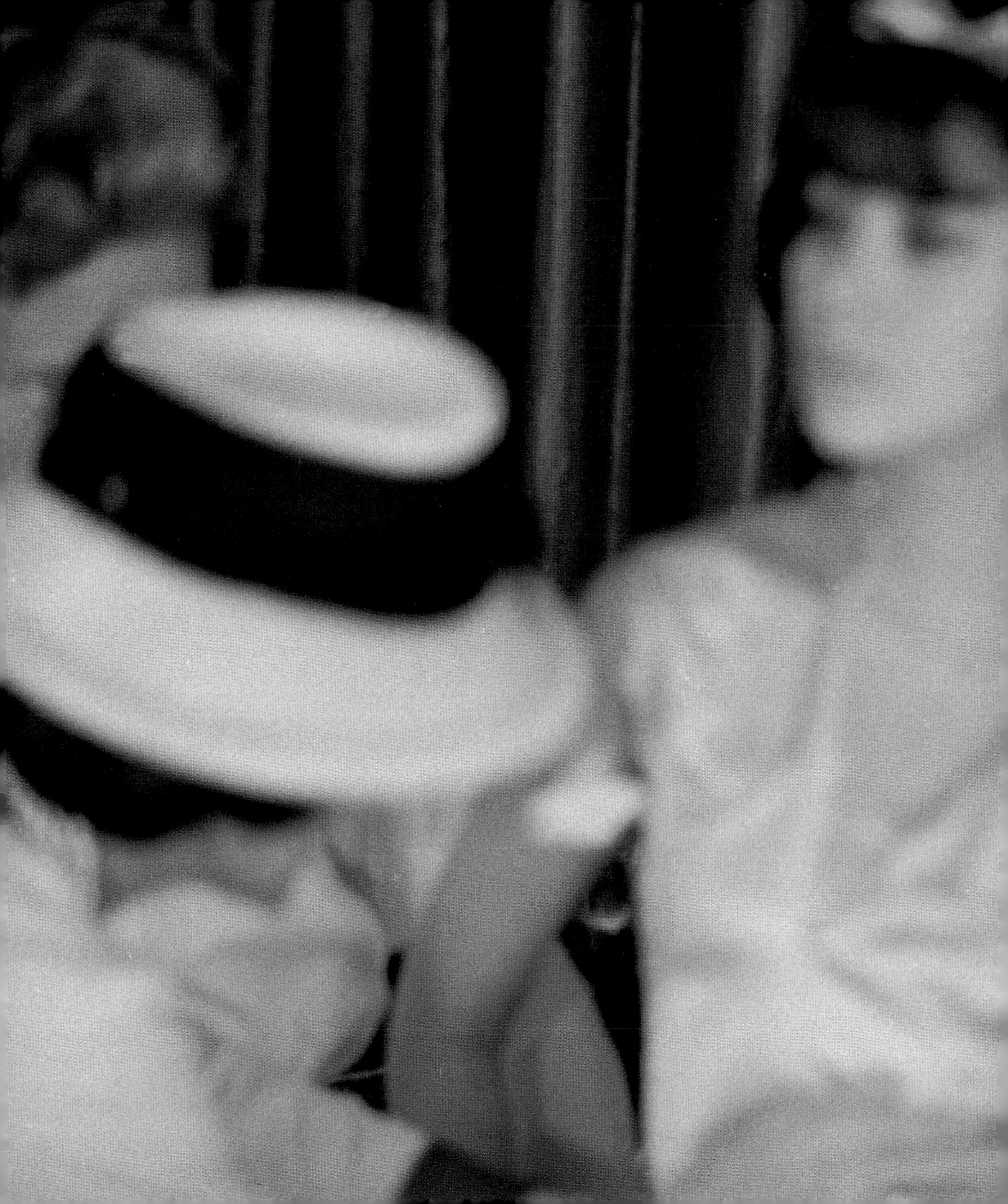

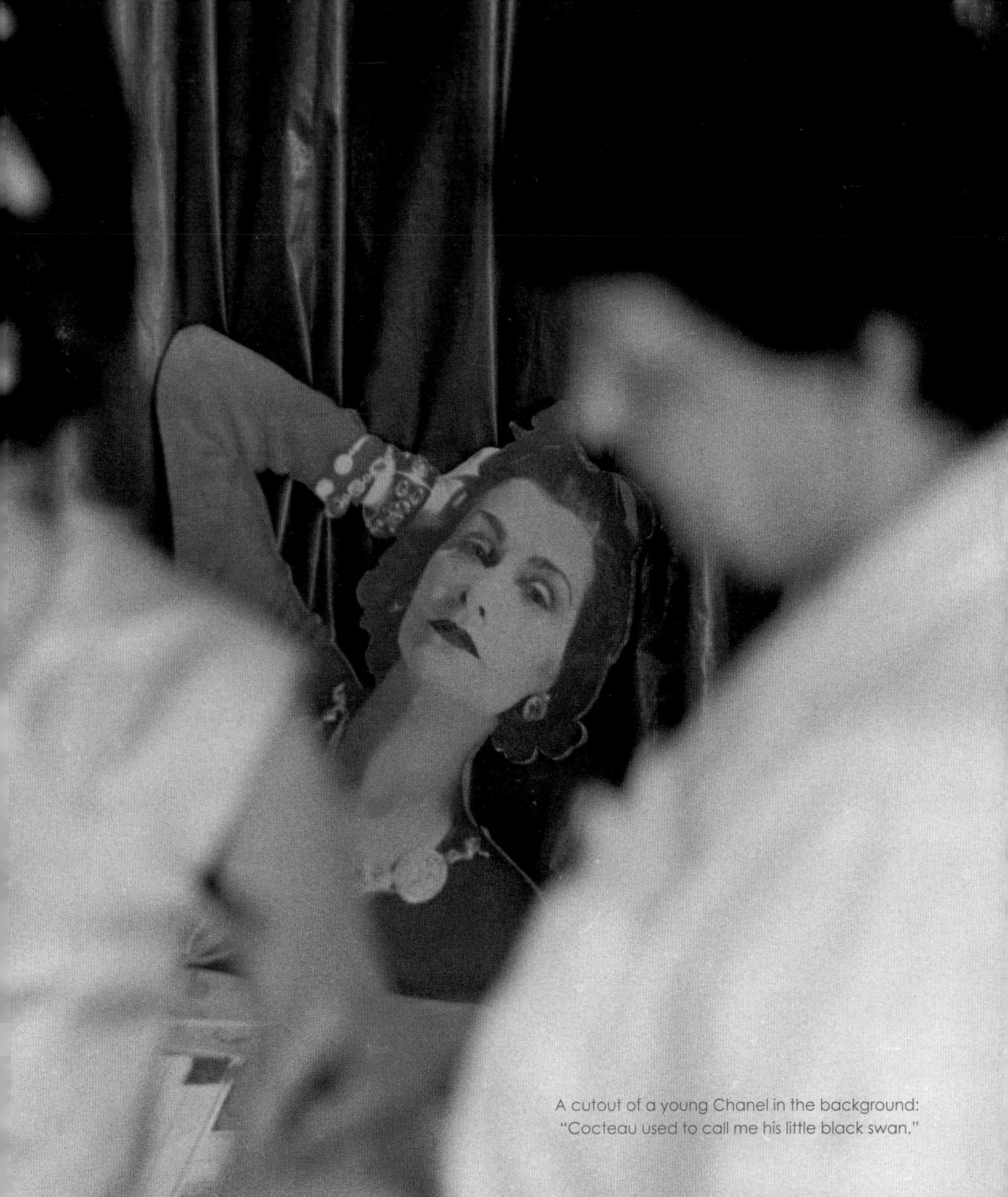

A cutout of a young Chanel in the background:
"Cocteau used to call me his little black swan."

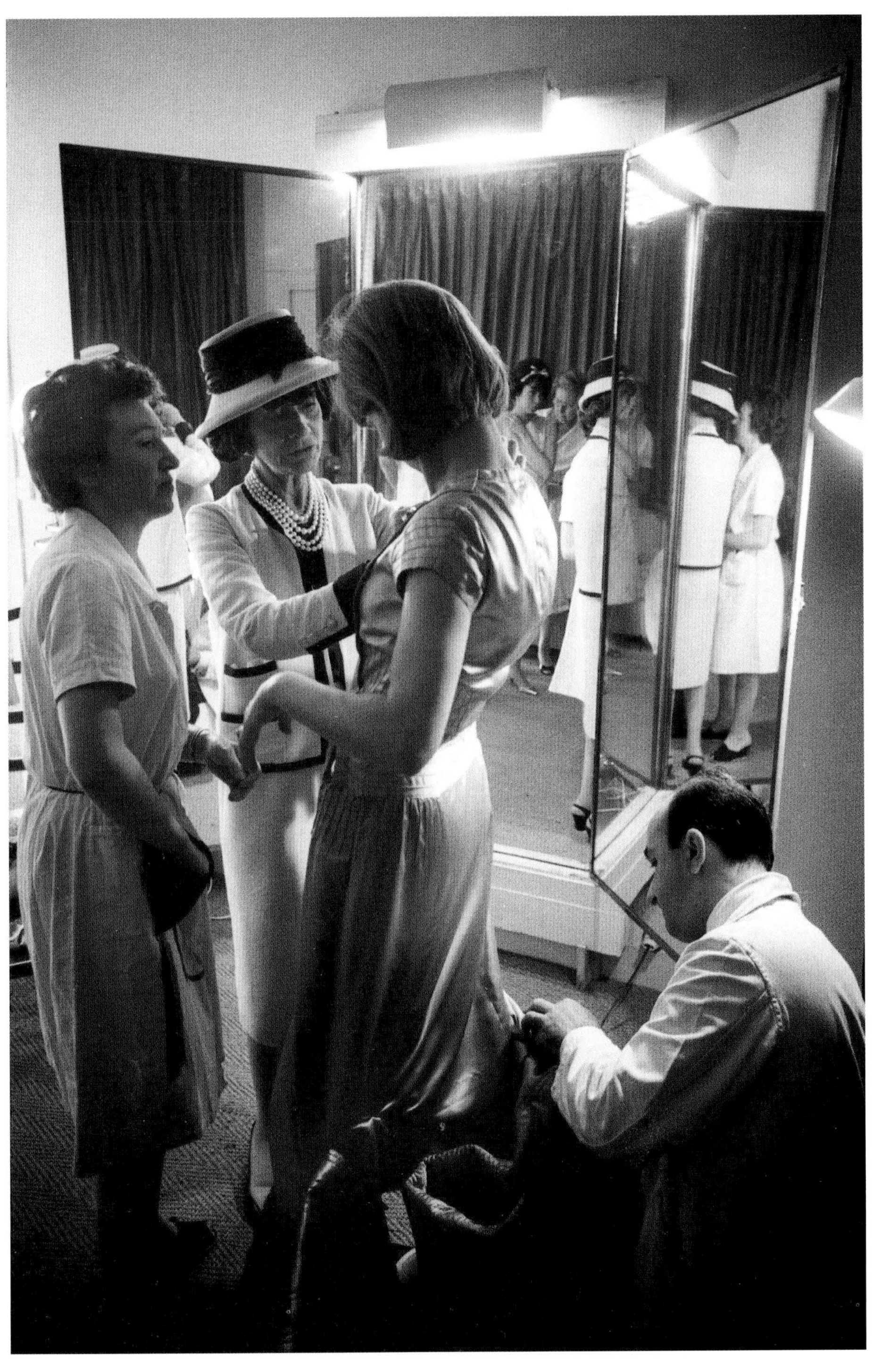

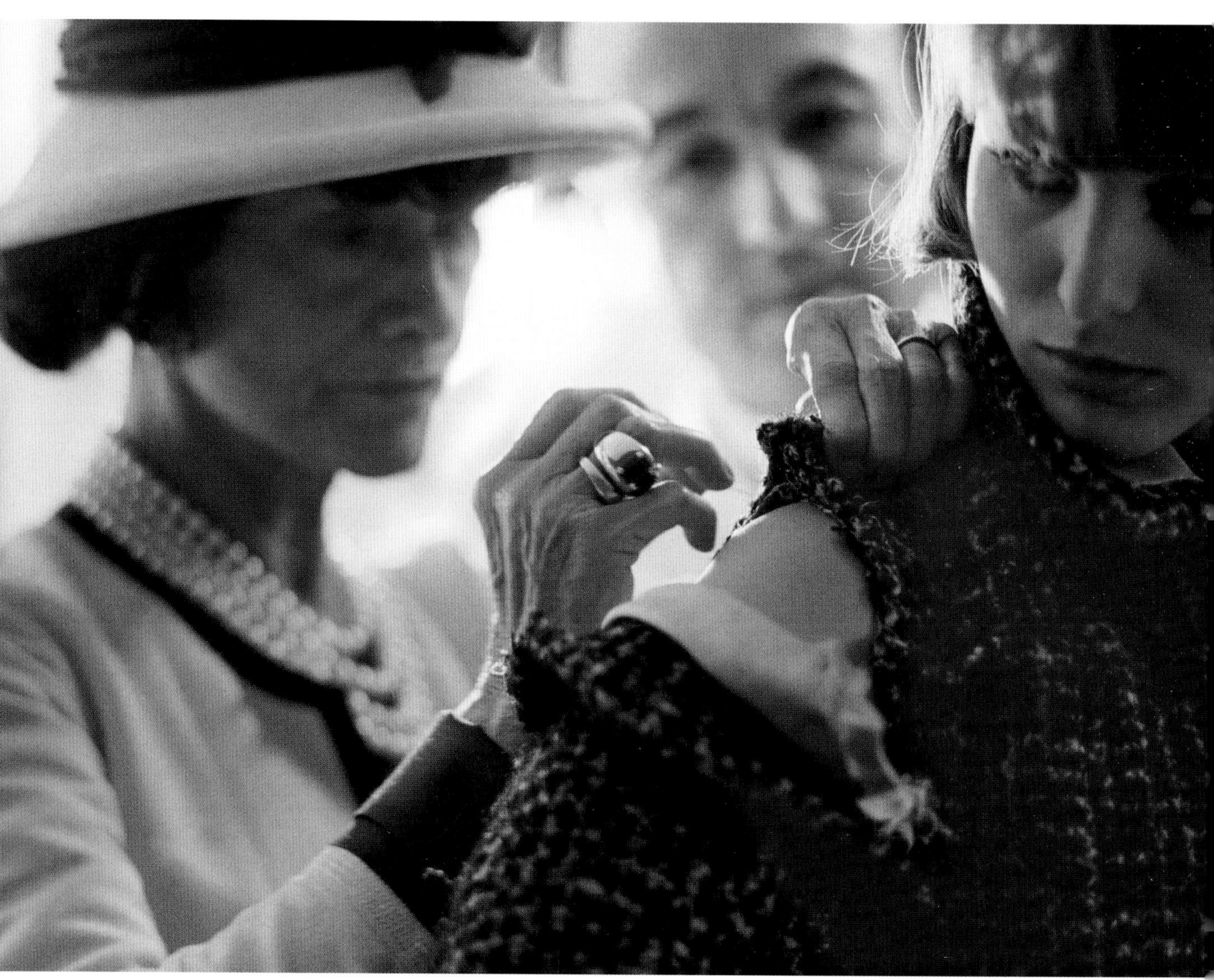

"My hands are sick, they have worked too much."

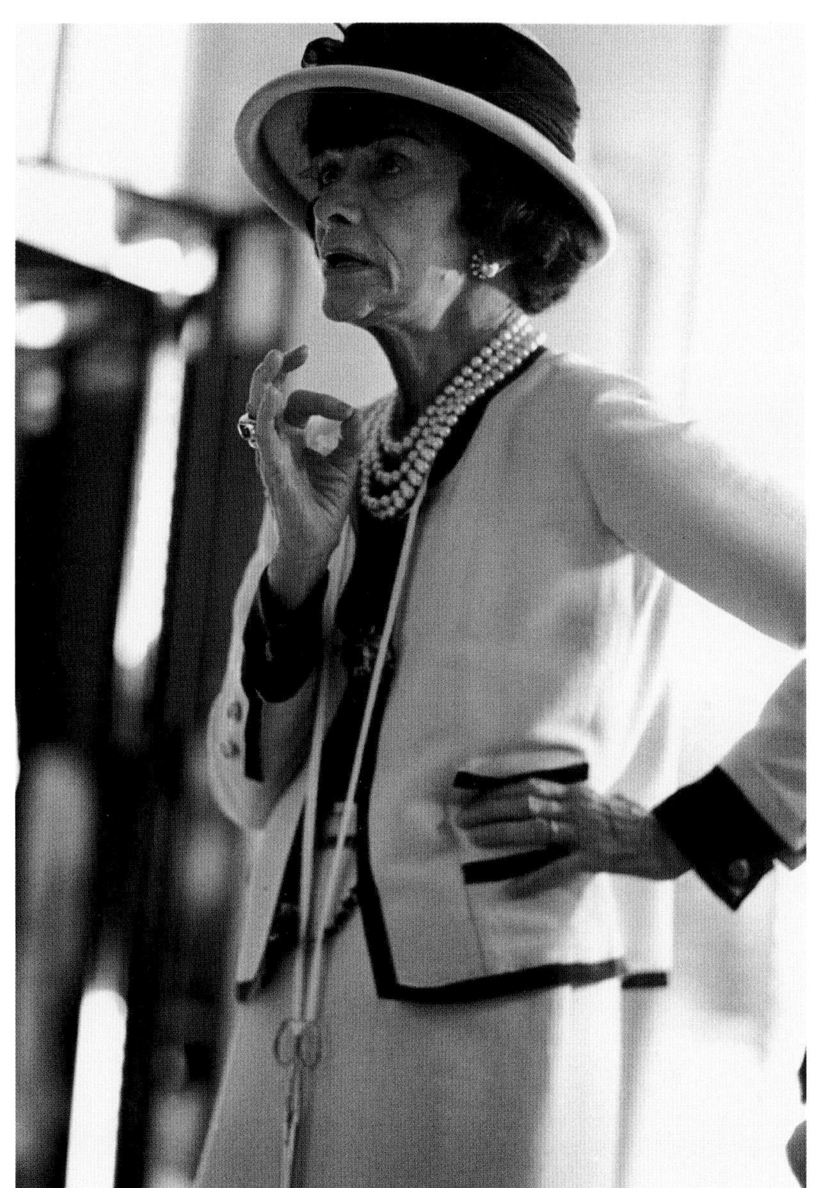

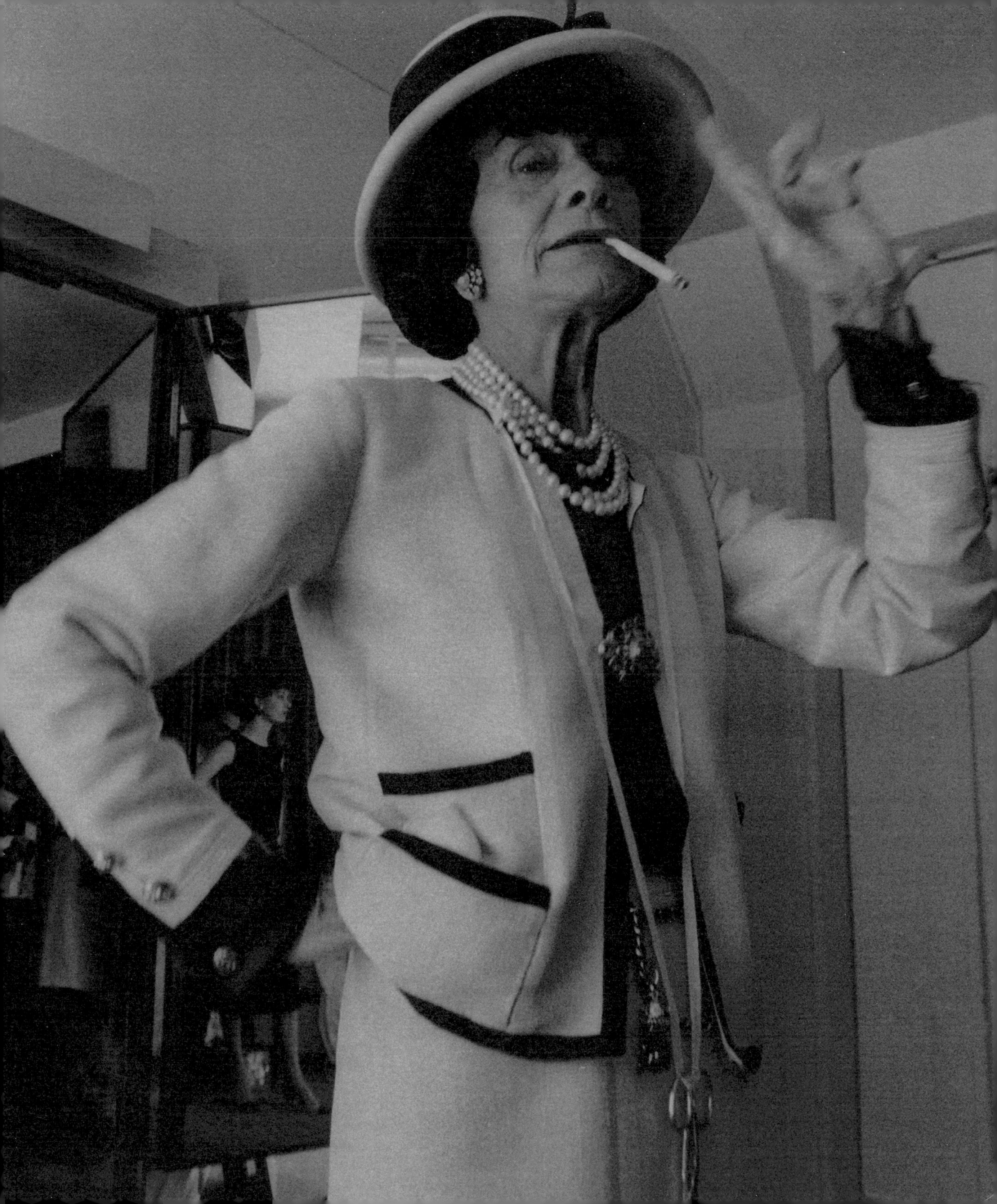

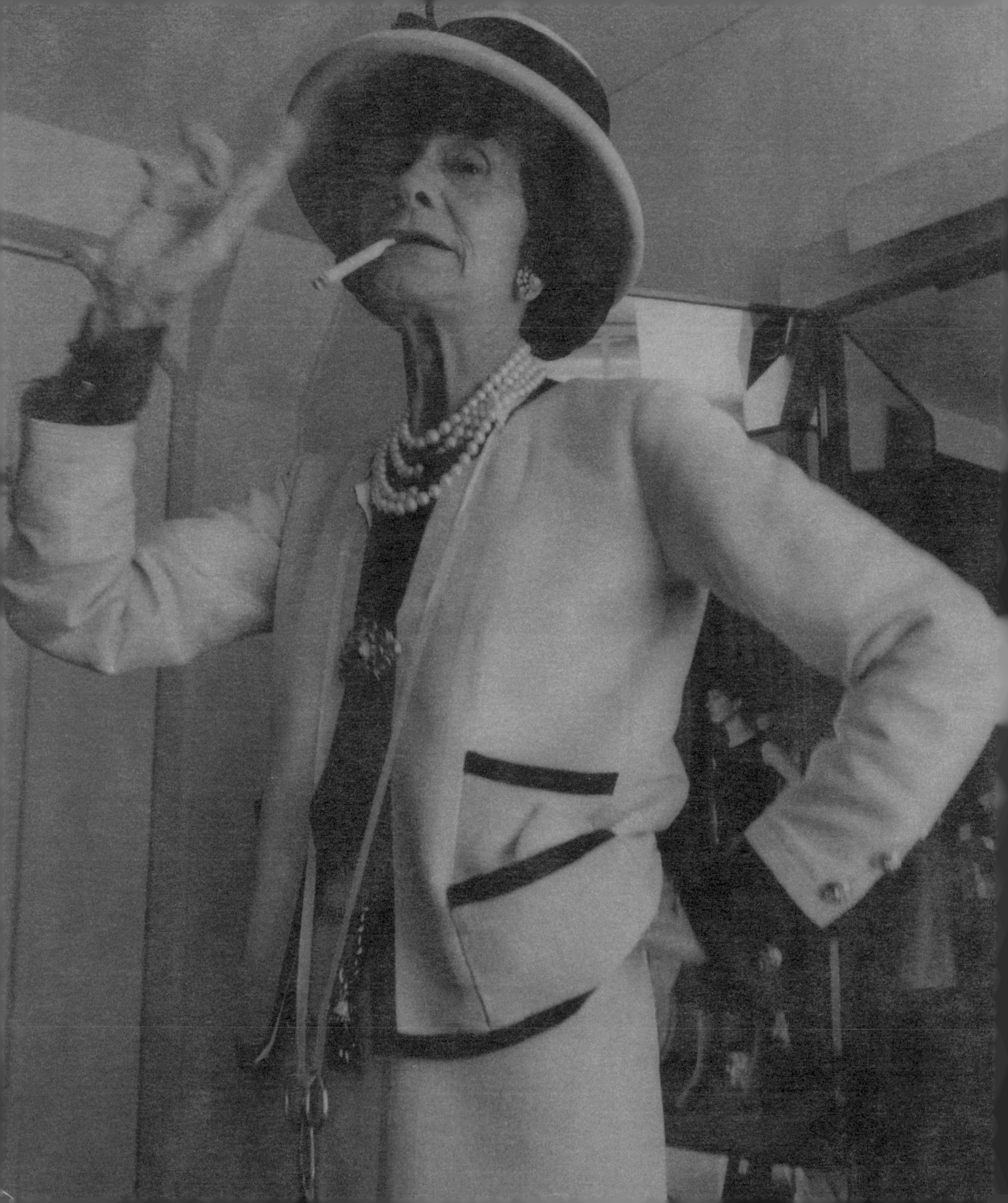

At seventy-nine, she still had impeccable posture and stood like a ballerina.

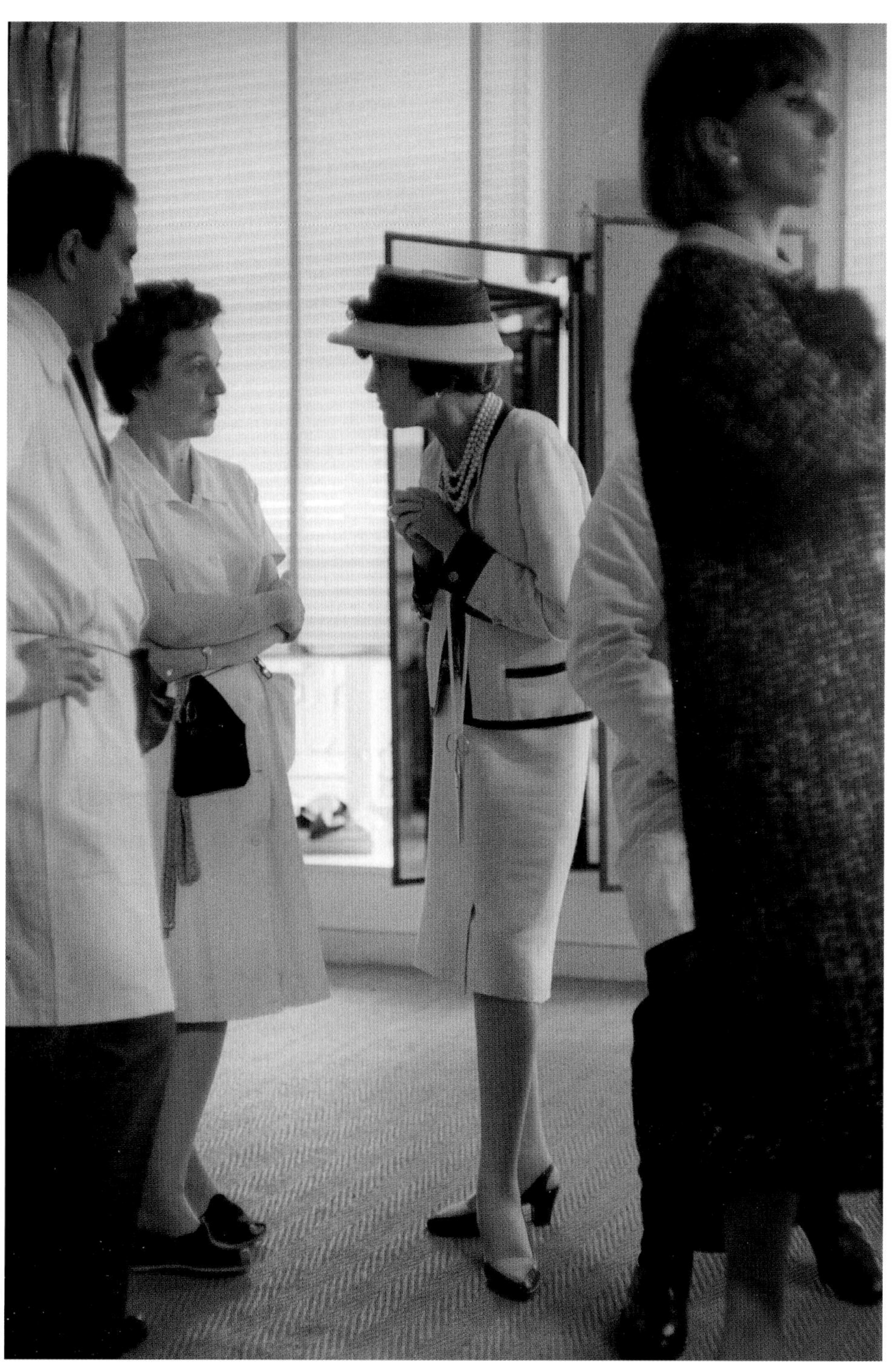

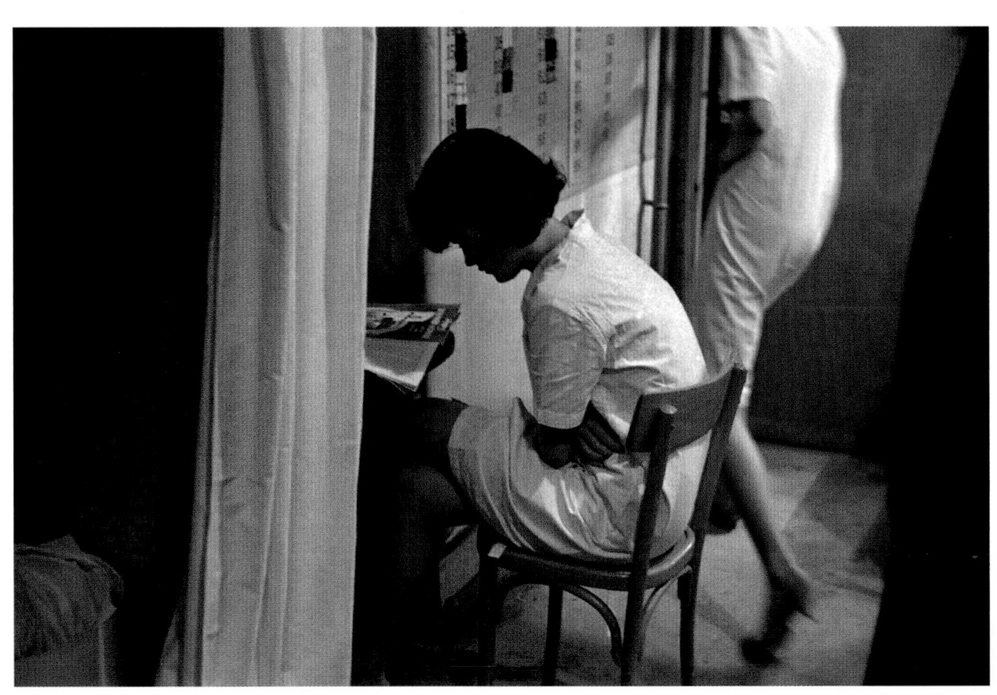

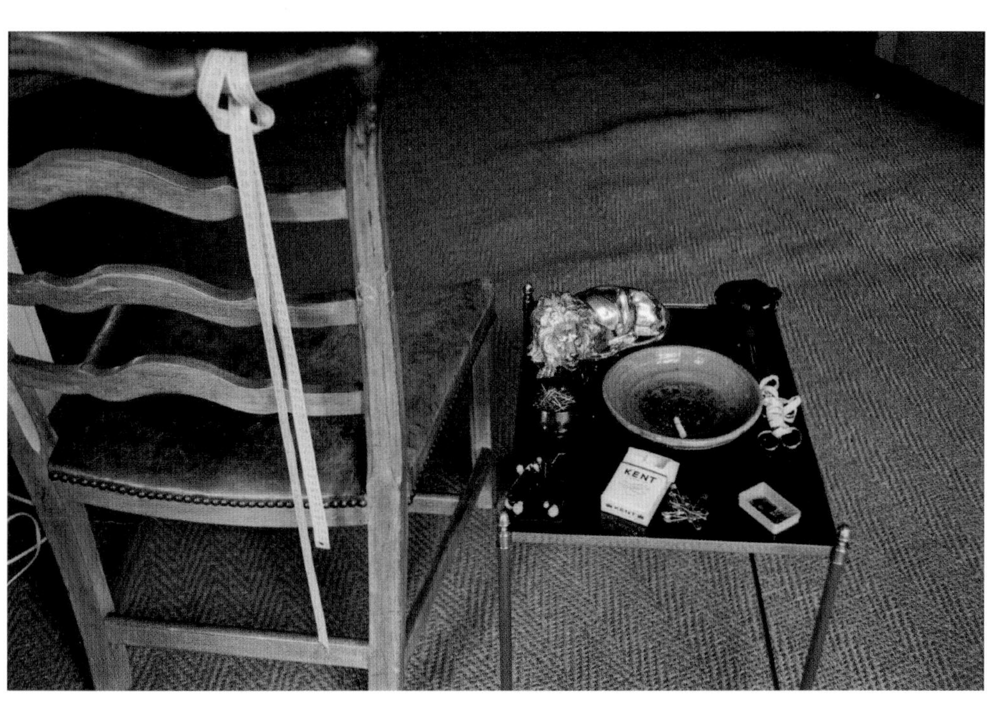
KENT

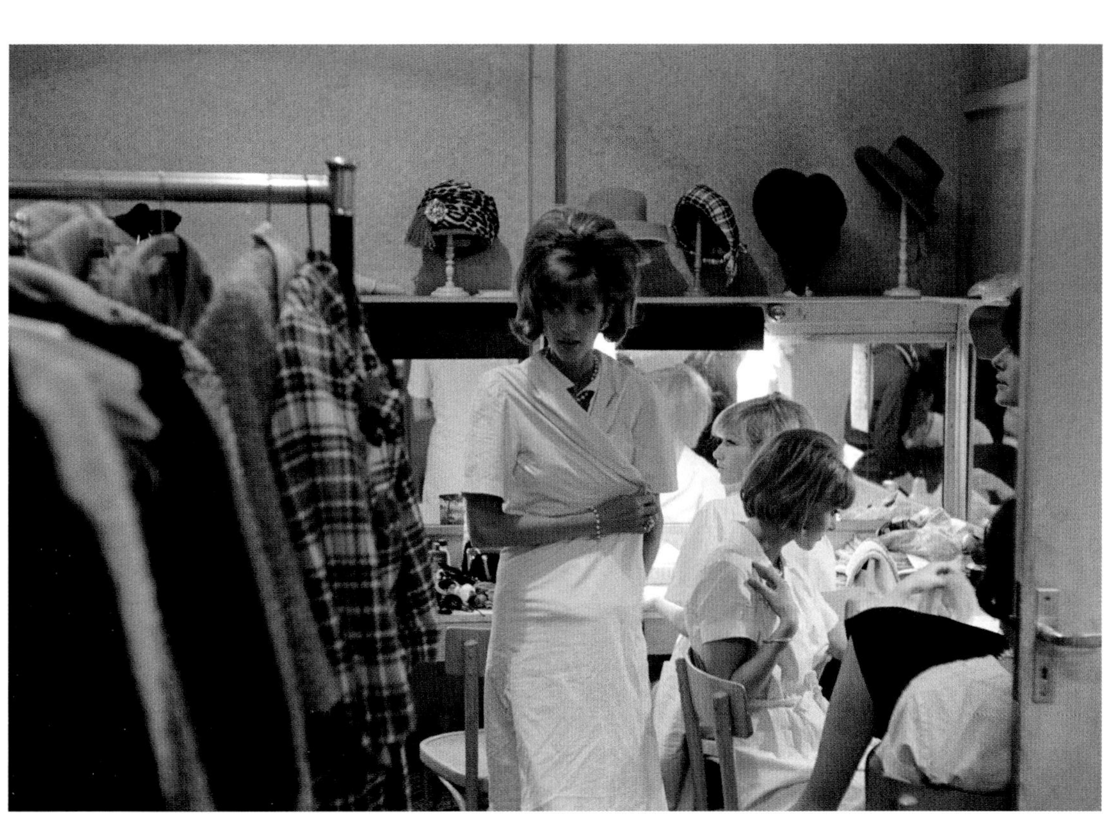

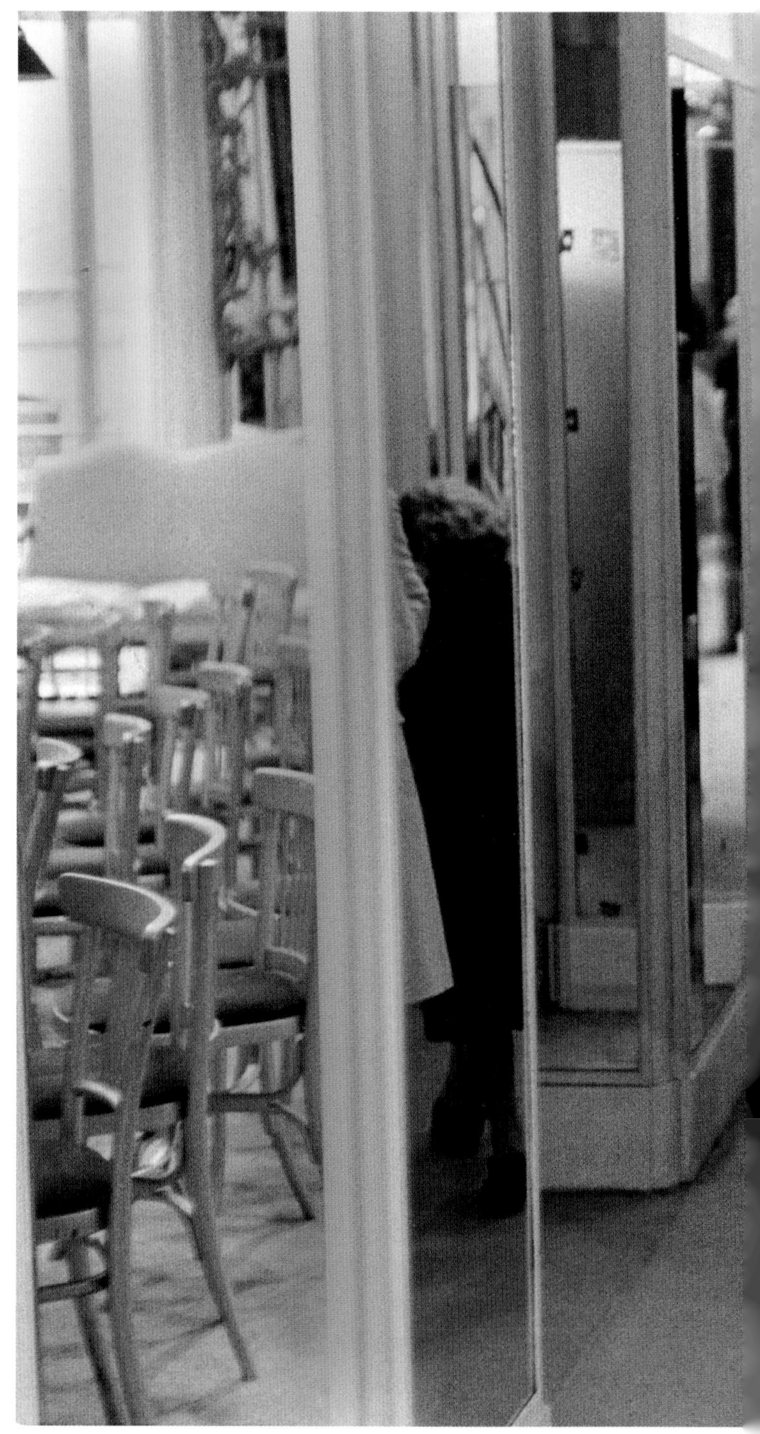

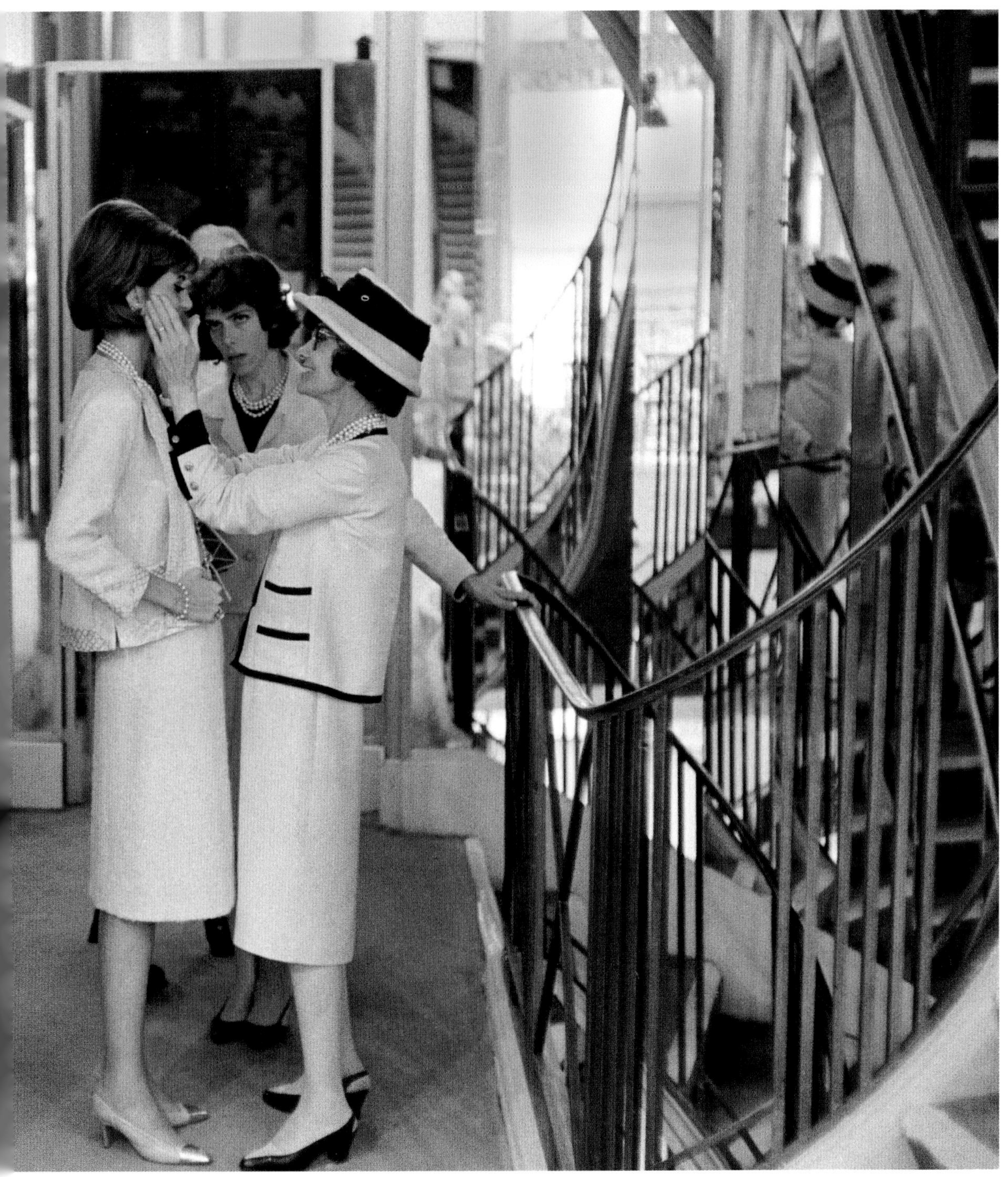

Dress shabbily and they remember the dress; dress impeccably and they remember the woman.

*Coco*

Art Buchwald, celebrated American columnist for the *International Herald Tribune*, and model Dorian Leigh arriving for the *défilé* (show) of the new collection.

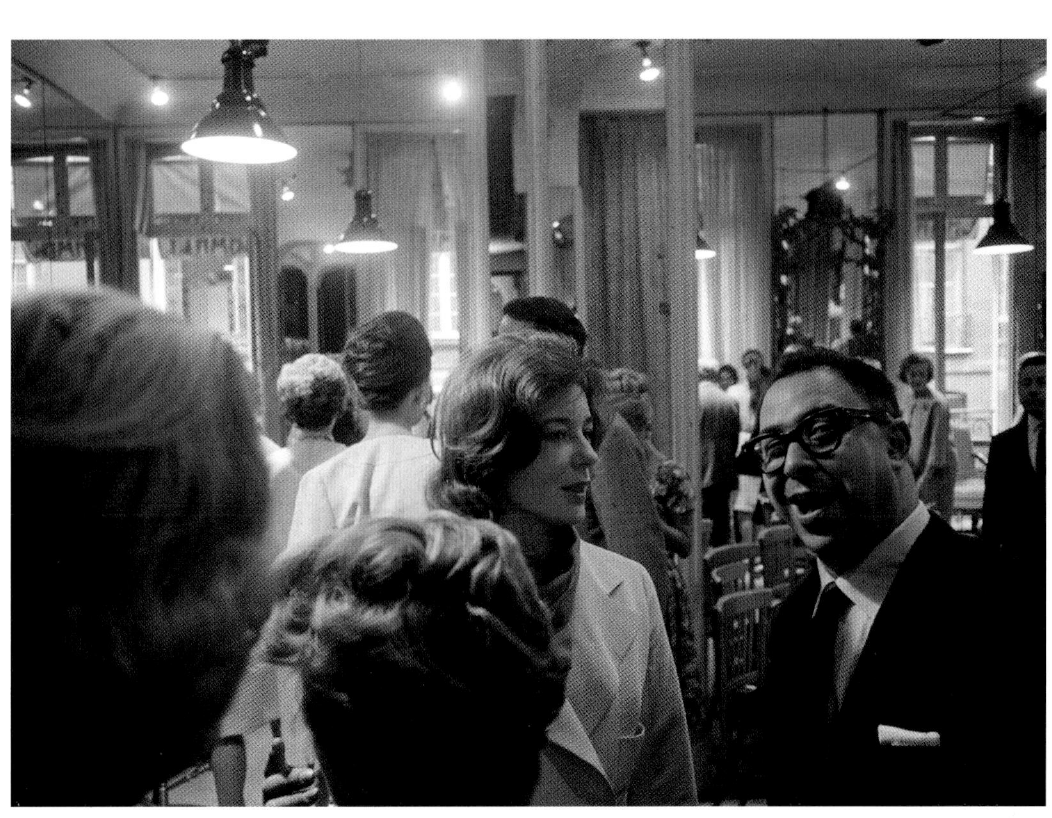

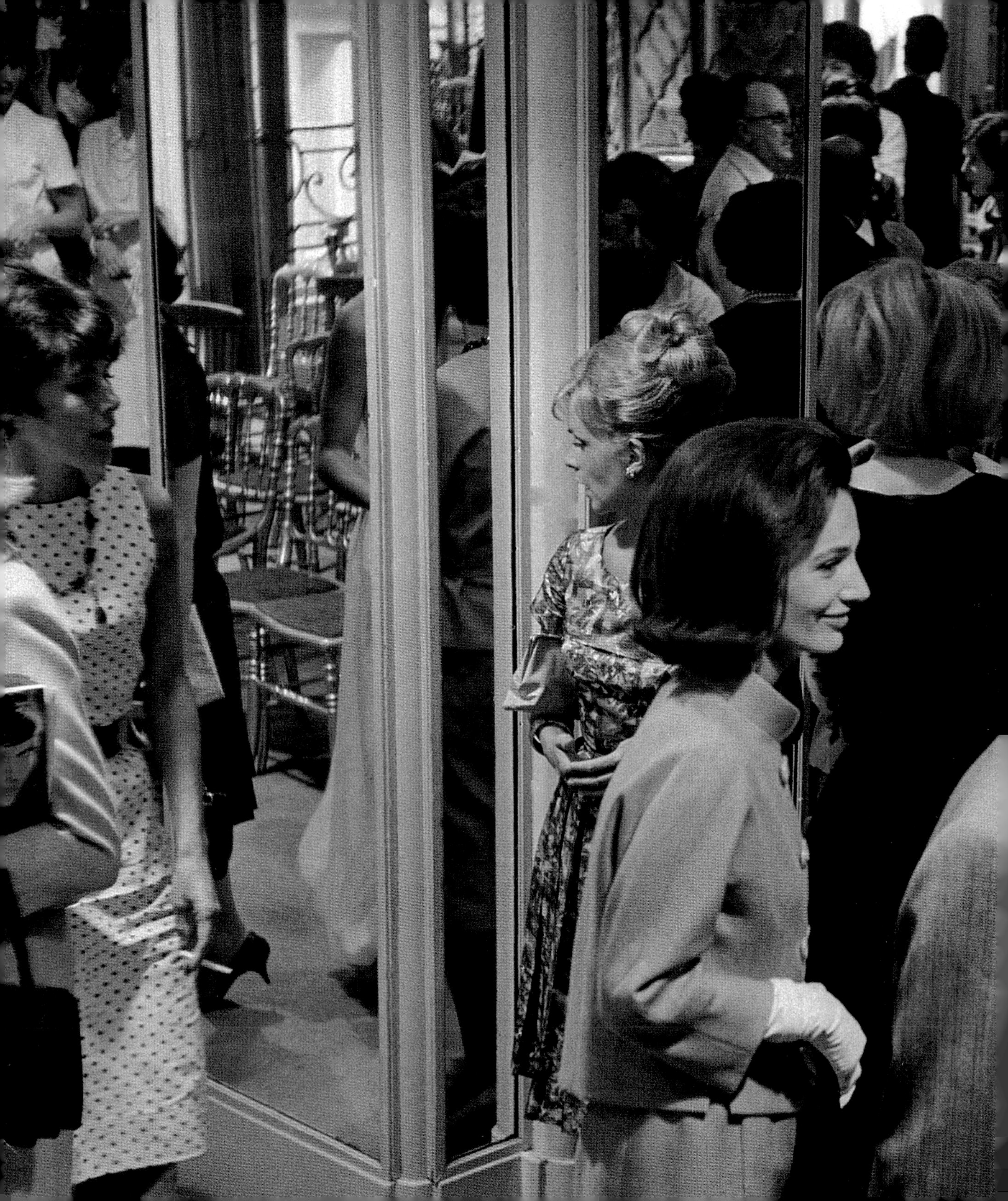

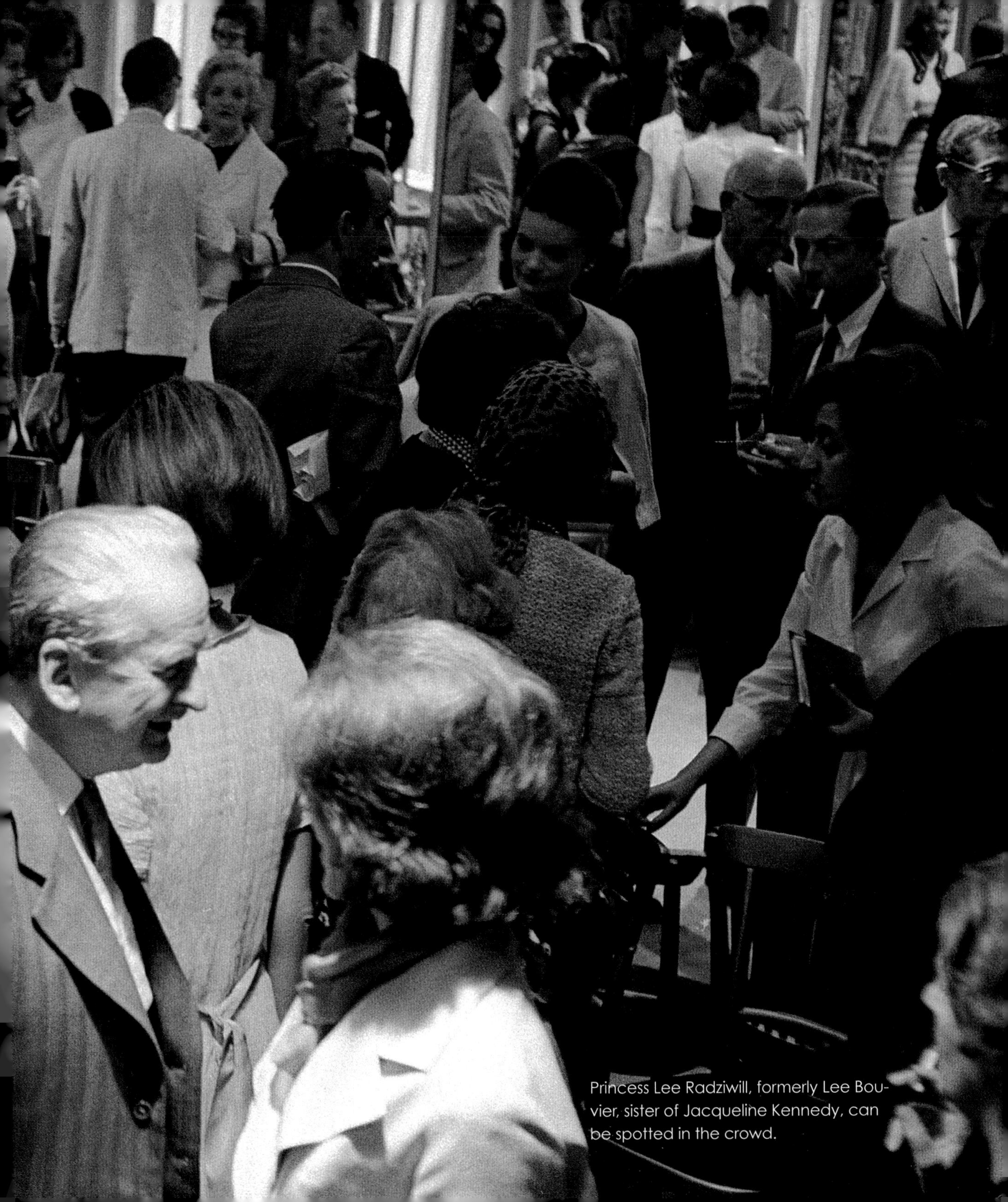

Princess Lee Radziwill, formerly Lee Bouvier, sister of Jacqueline Kennedy, can be spotted in the crowd.

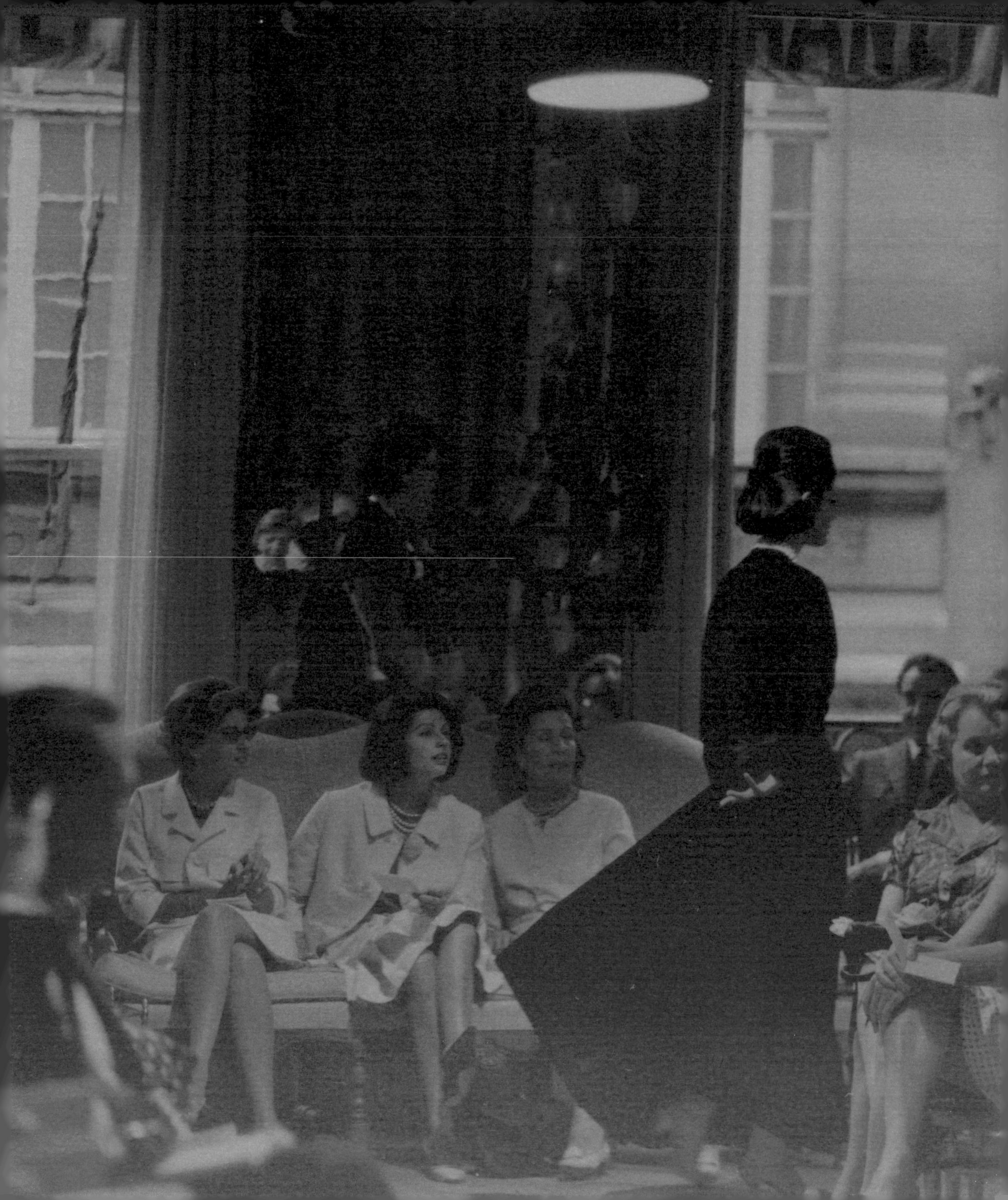

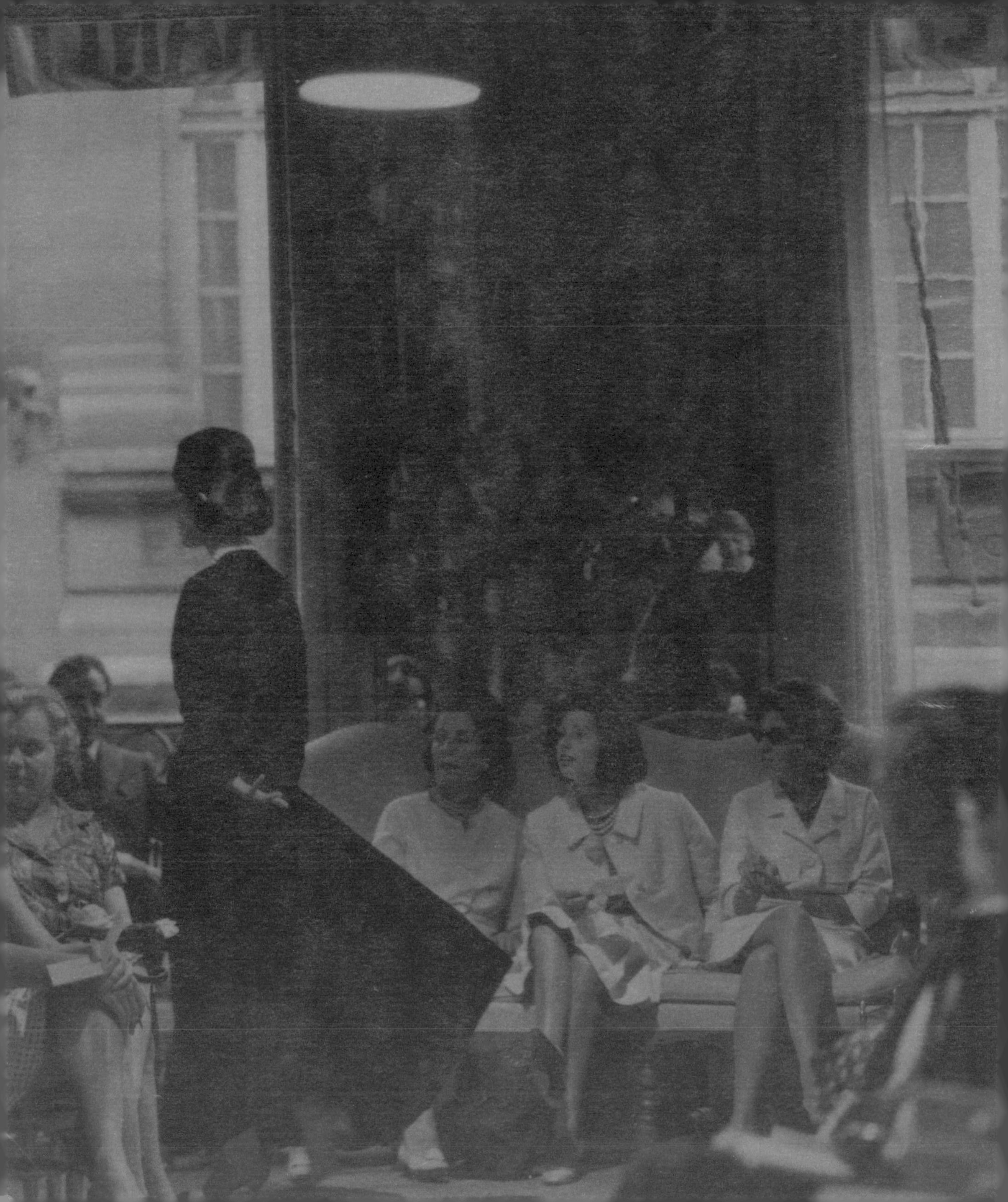

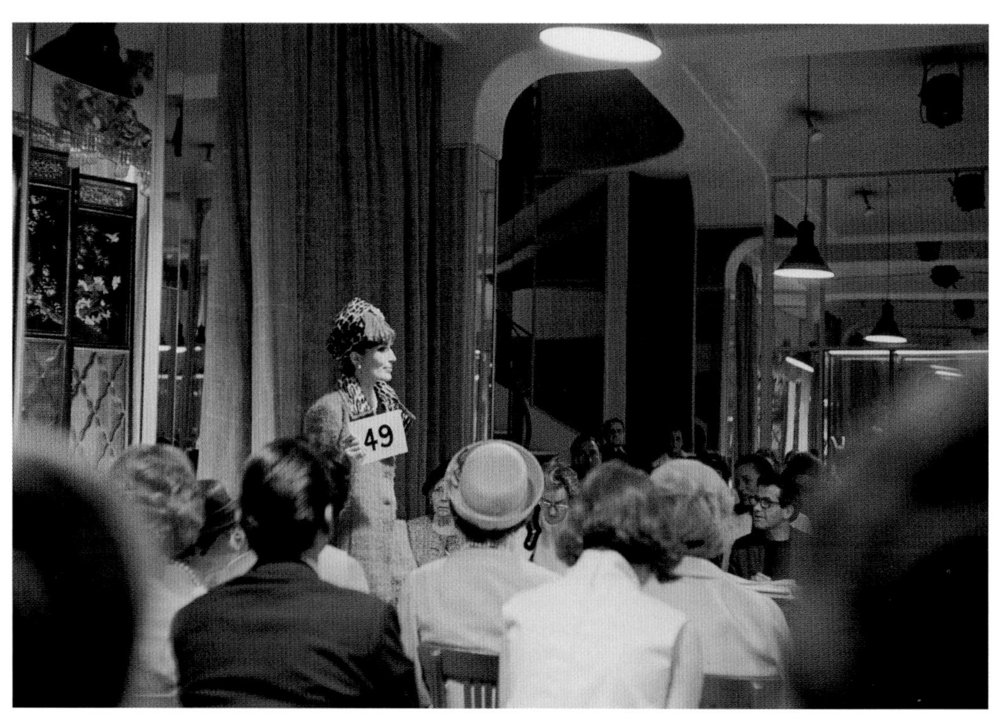


As the models first stepped out, confidently holding their numbers, there was a sense of anticipation and anxiety in the air.

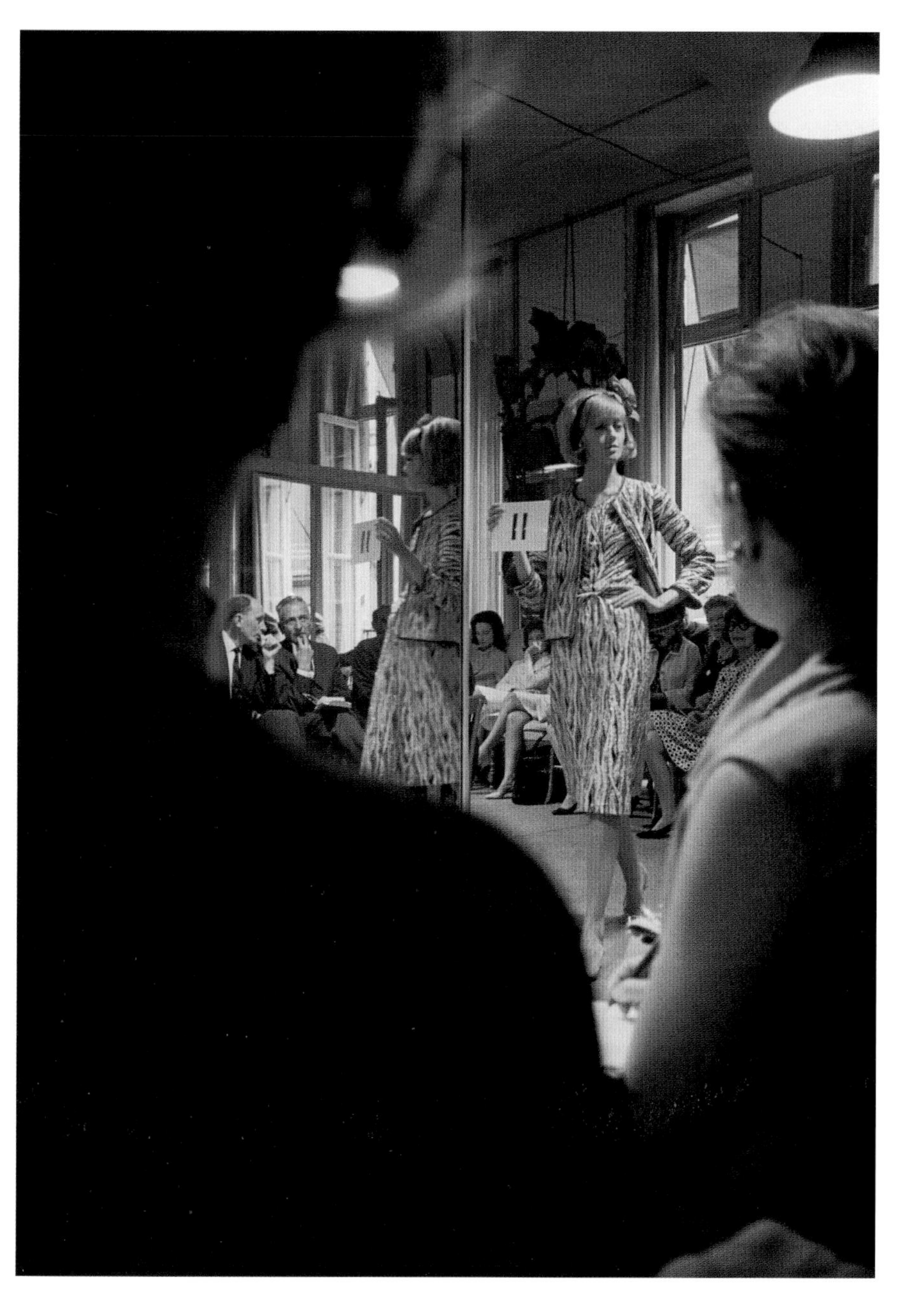
11

Mademoiselle was famous for watching the *défilé* (show), sitting out of sight on the stairs and observing the crowd's reaction through the kaleidoscopic mirrors.

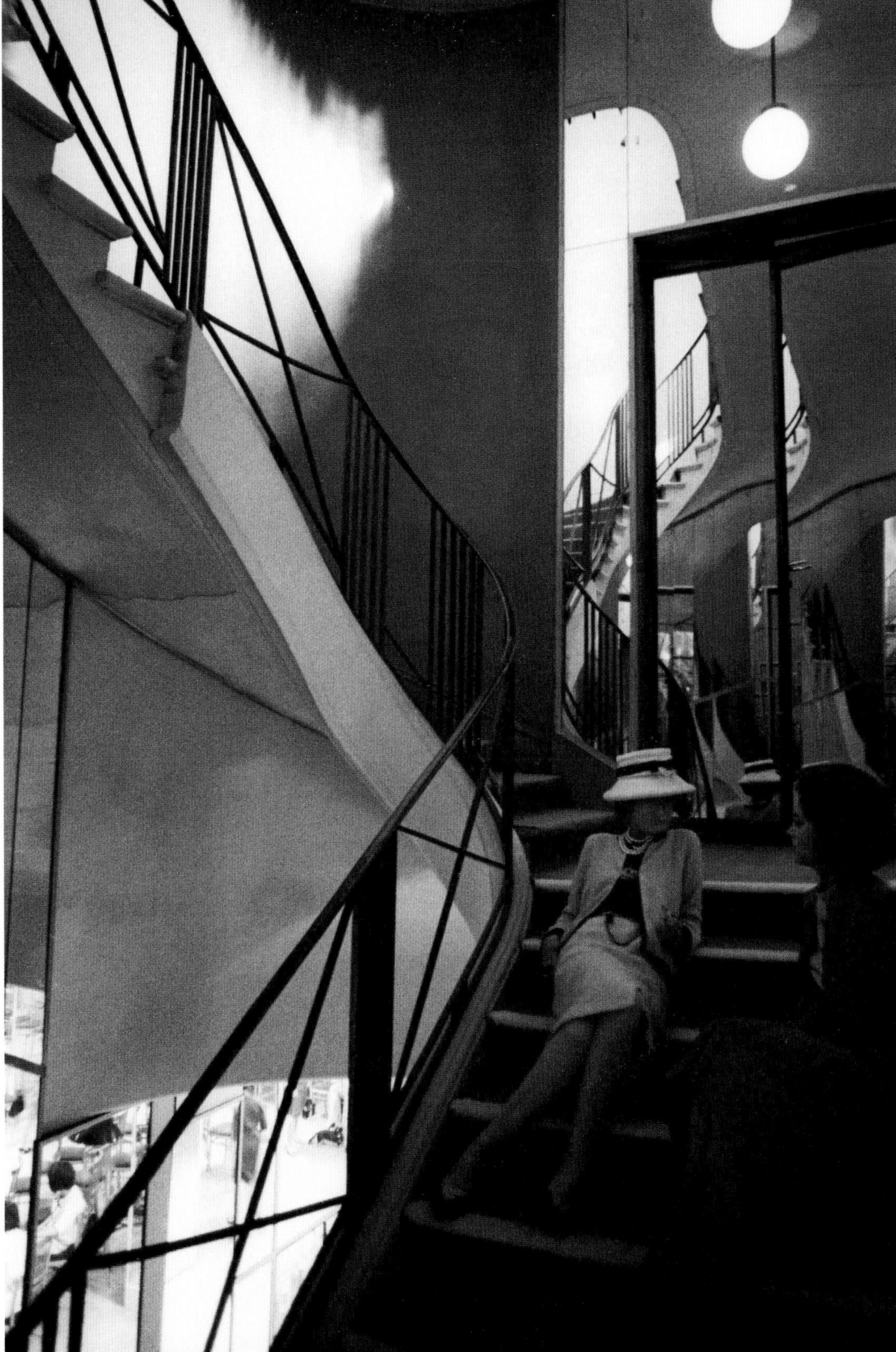

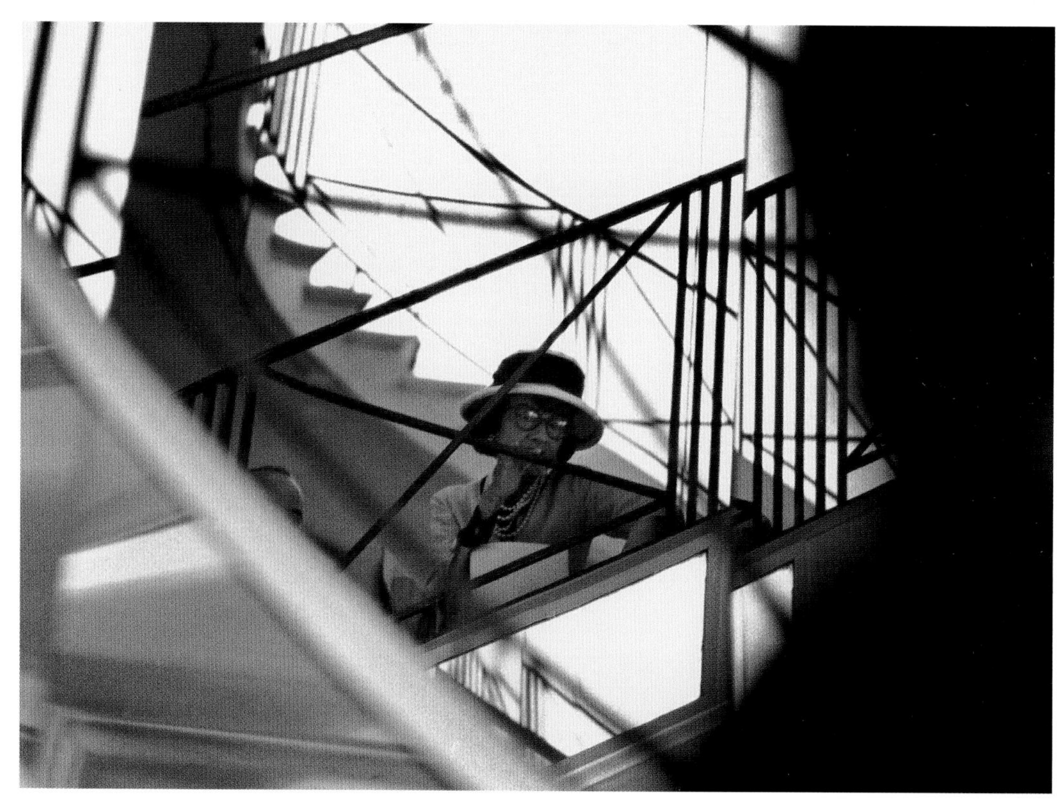

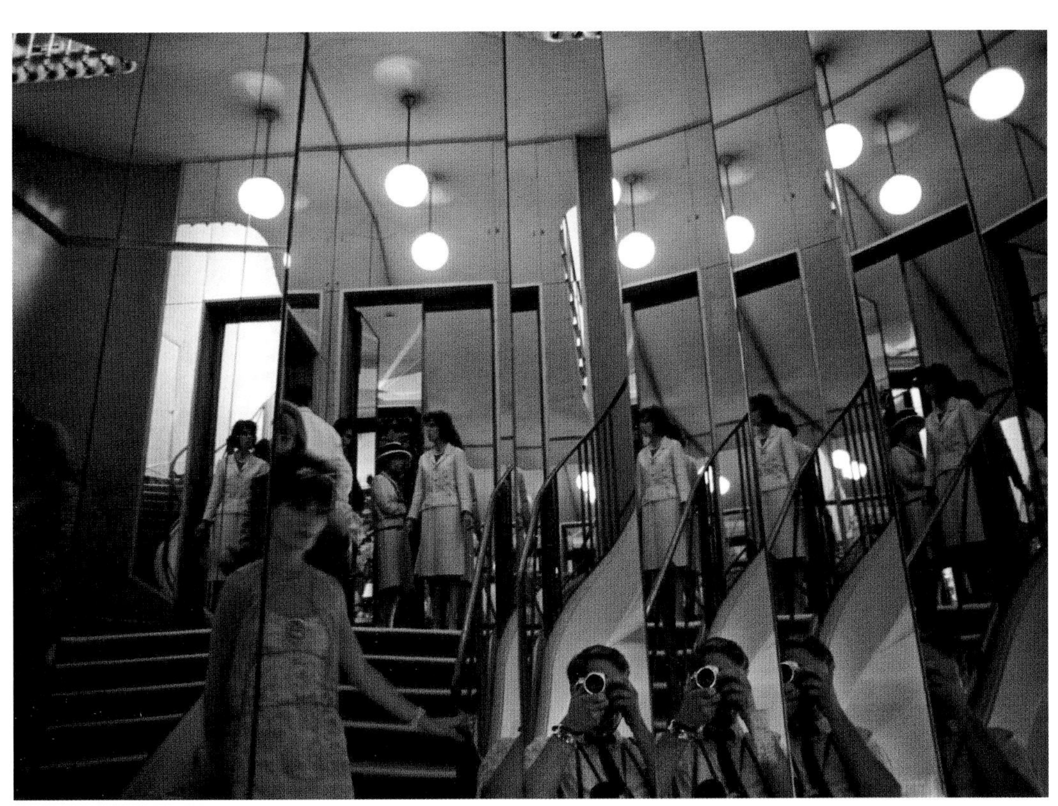

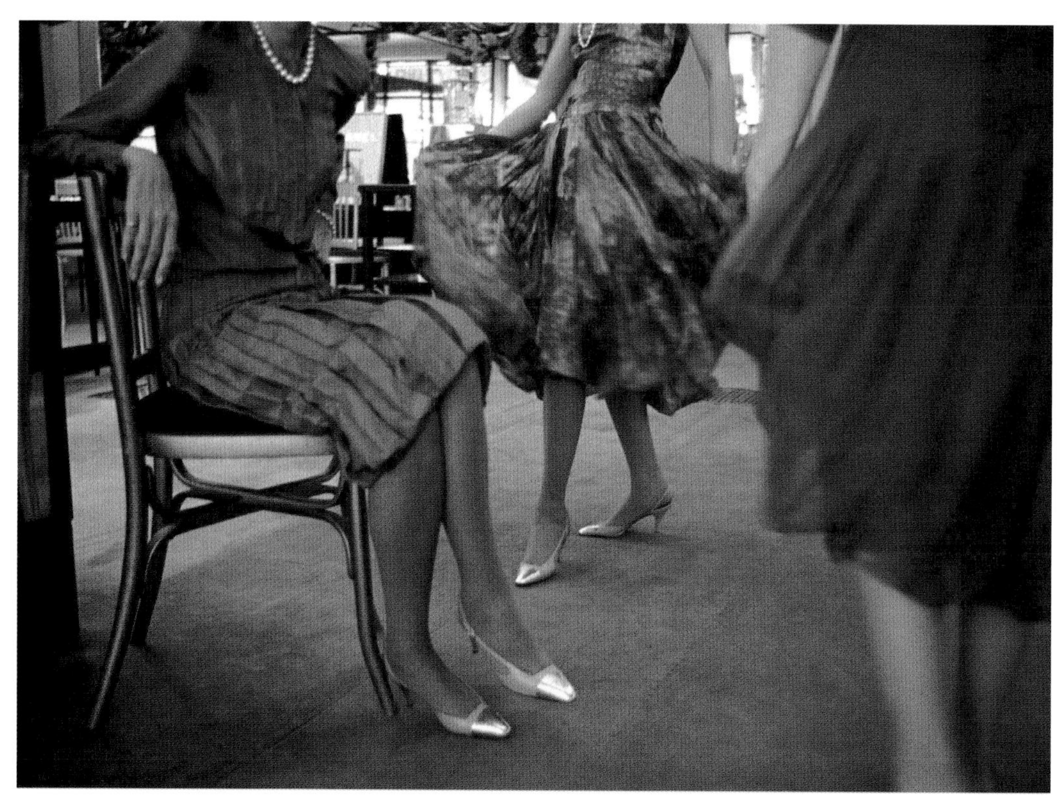

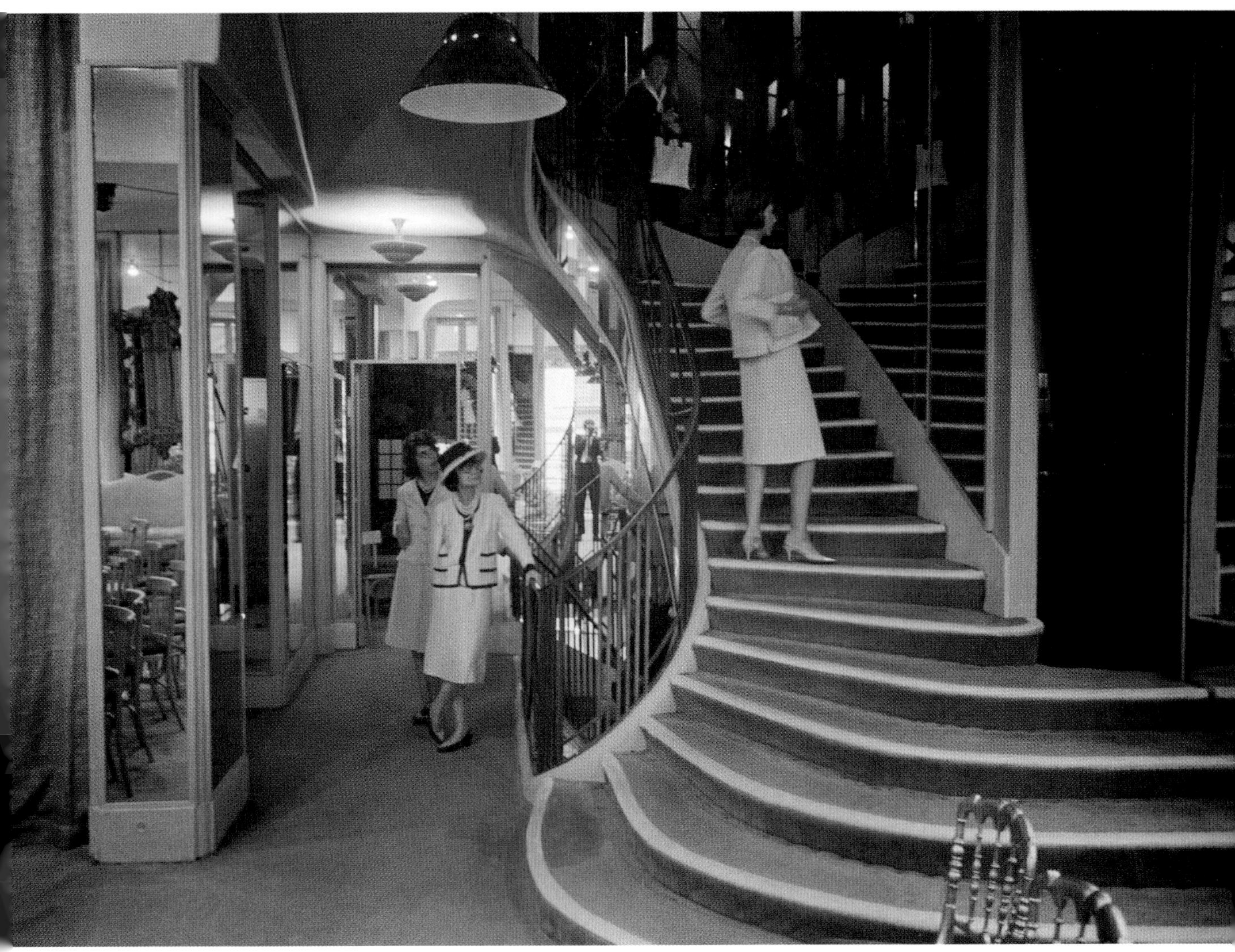

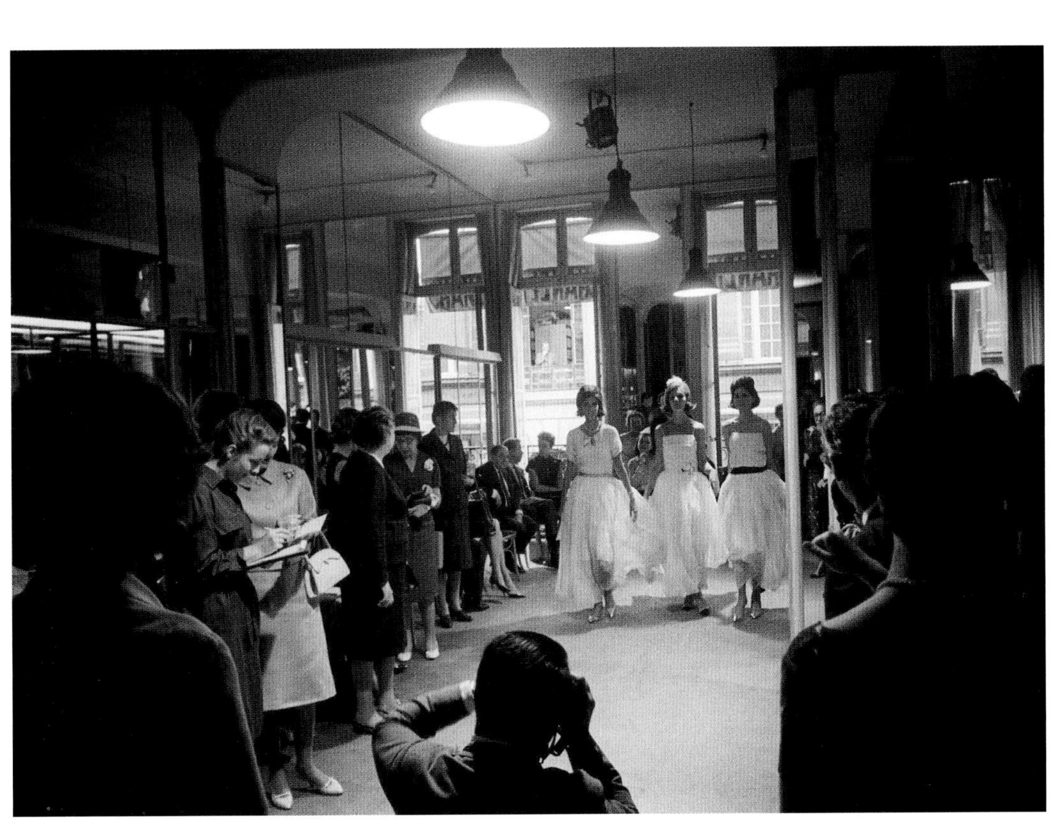

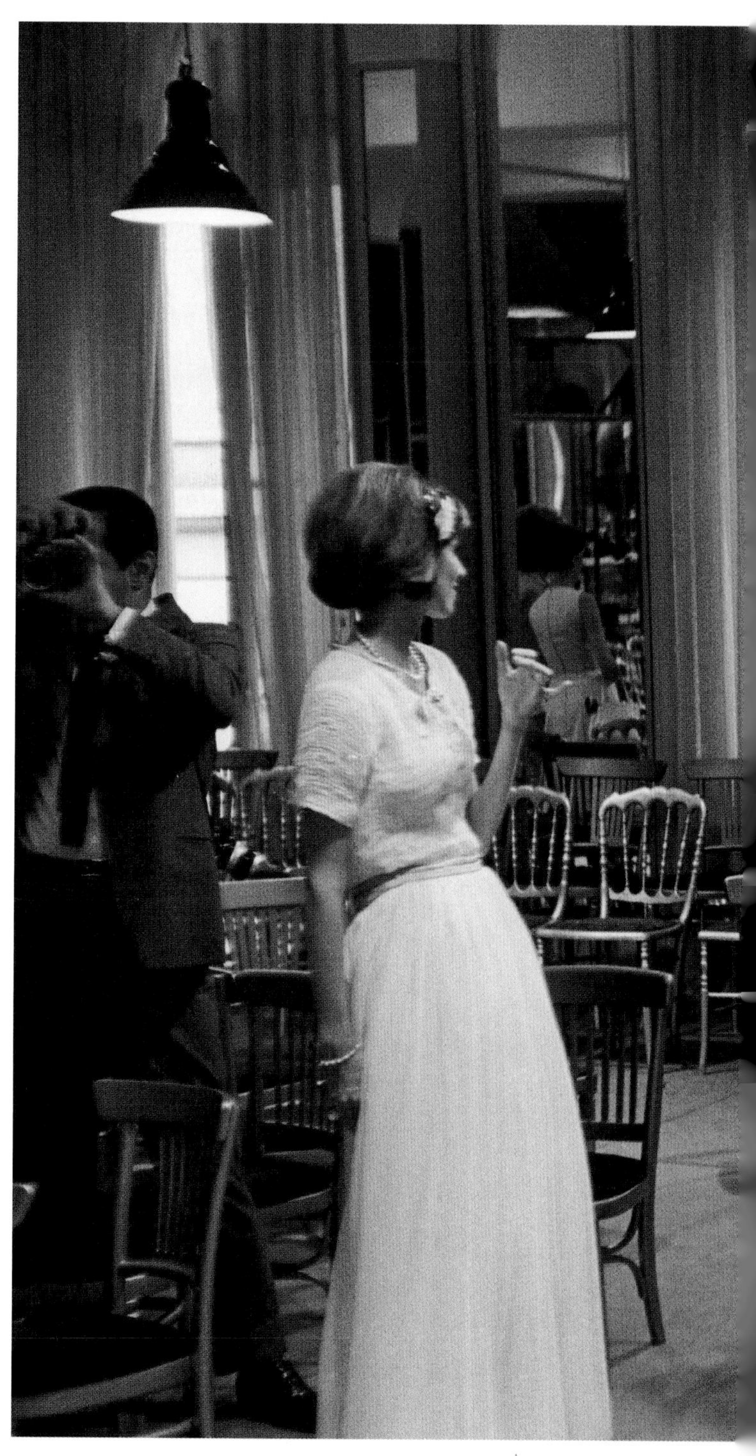

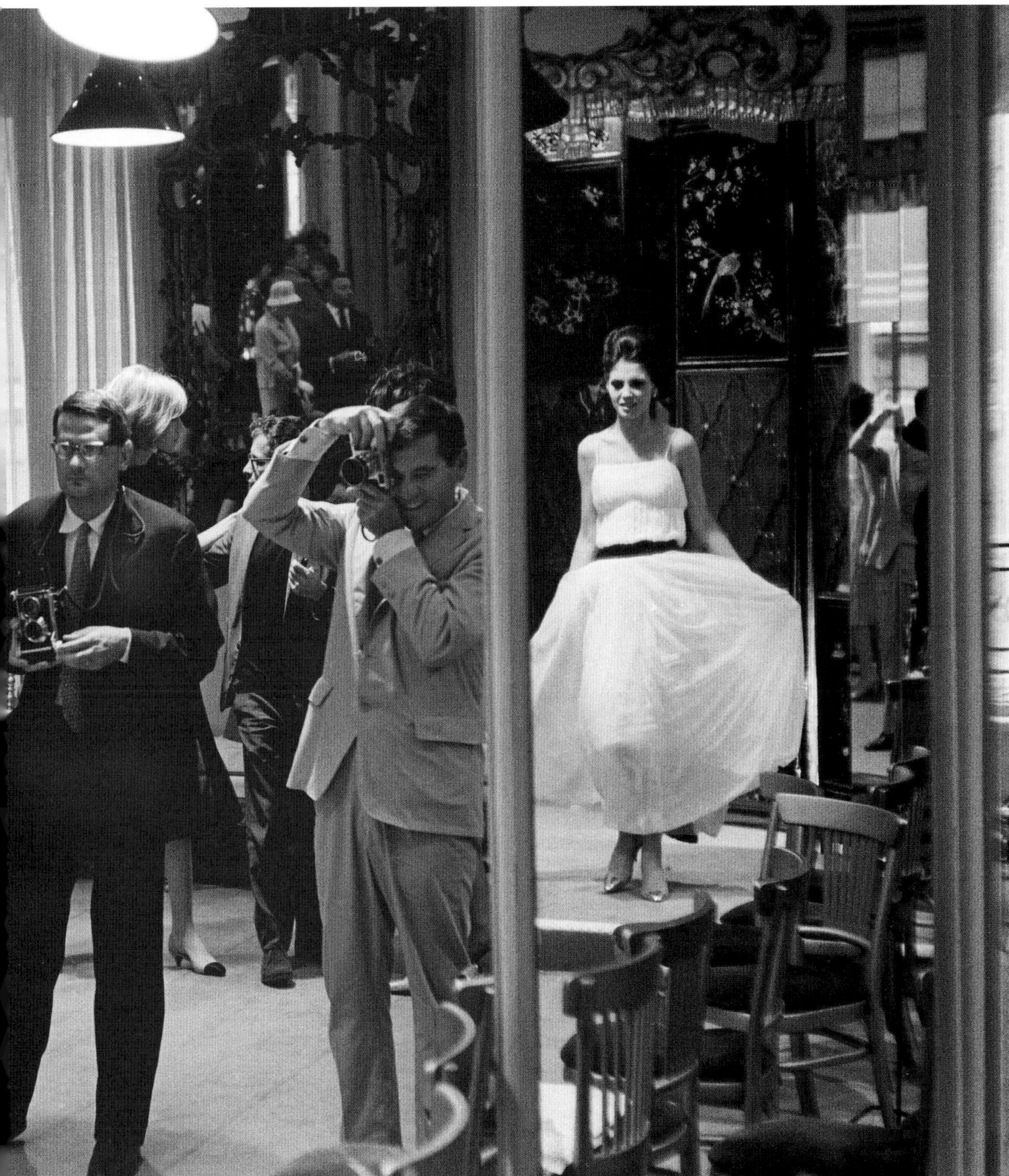

Fashion illustrators getting a closer look at the models after the show.

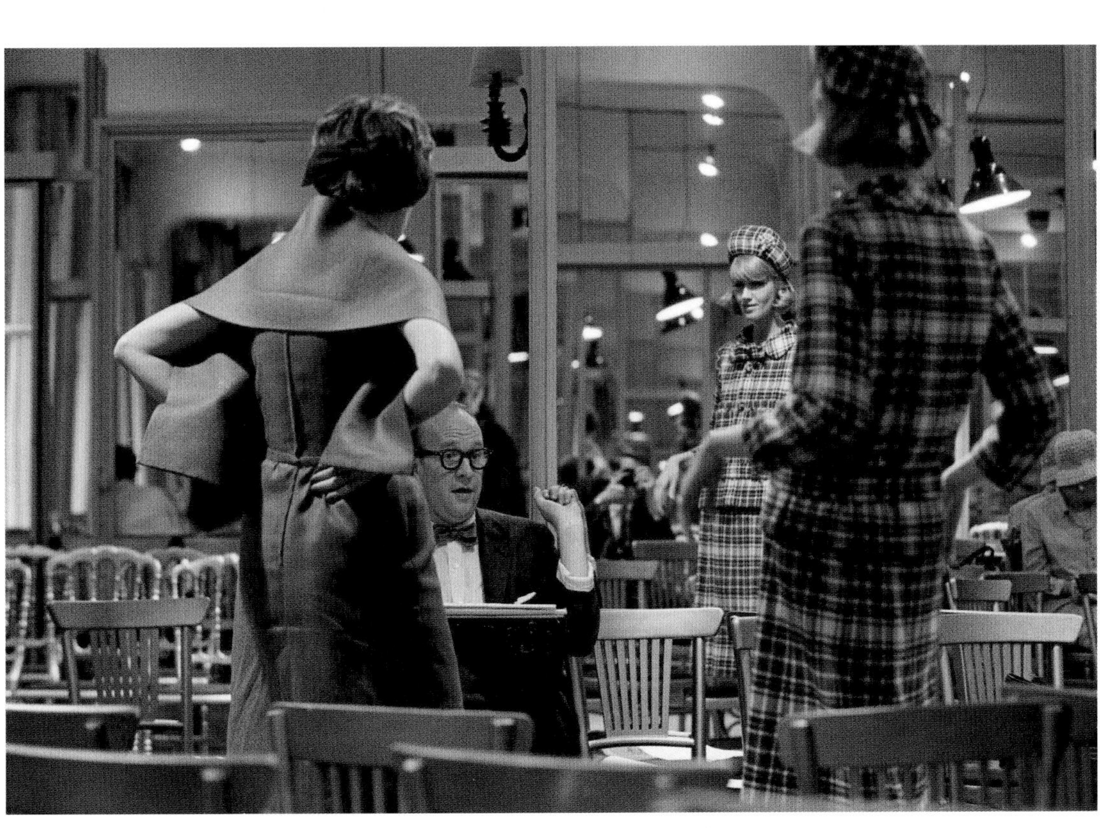

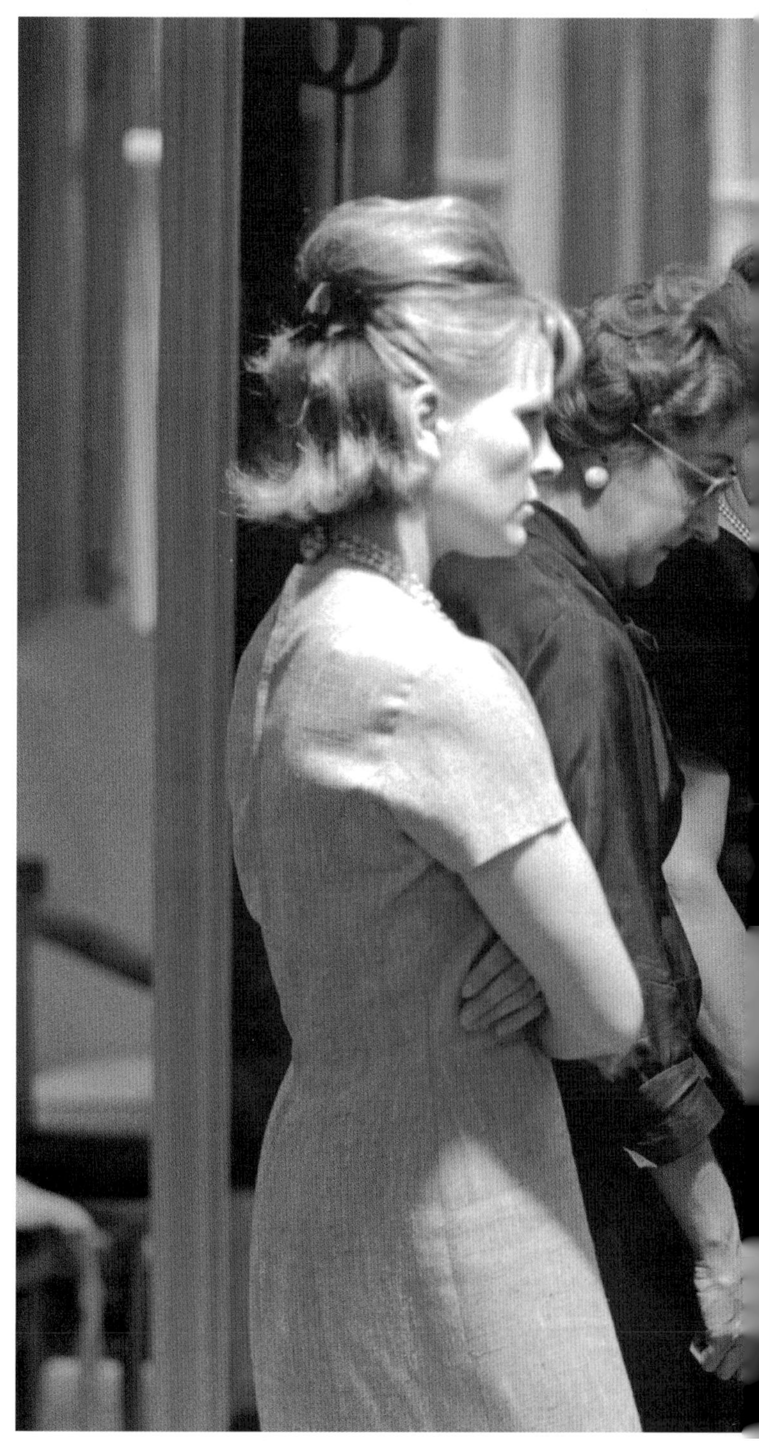

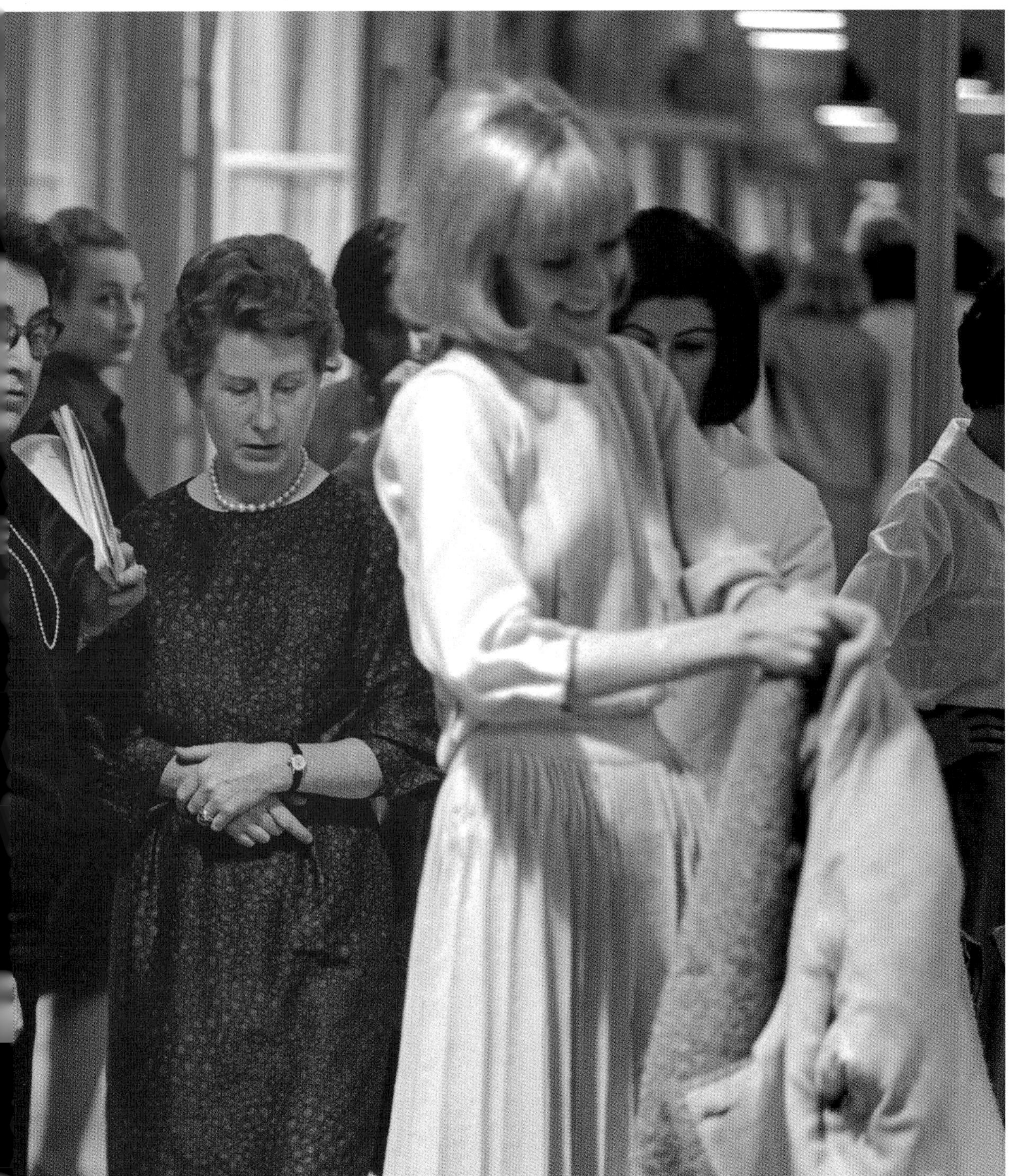

Fashion editors scrutinizing this season's design.

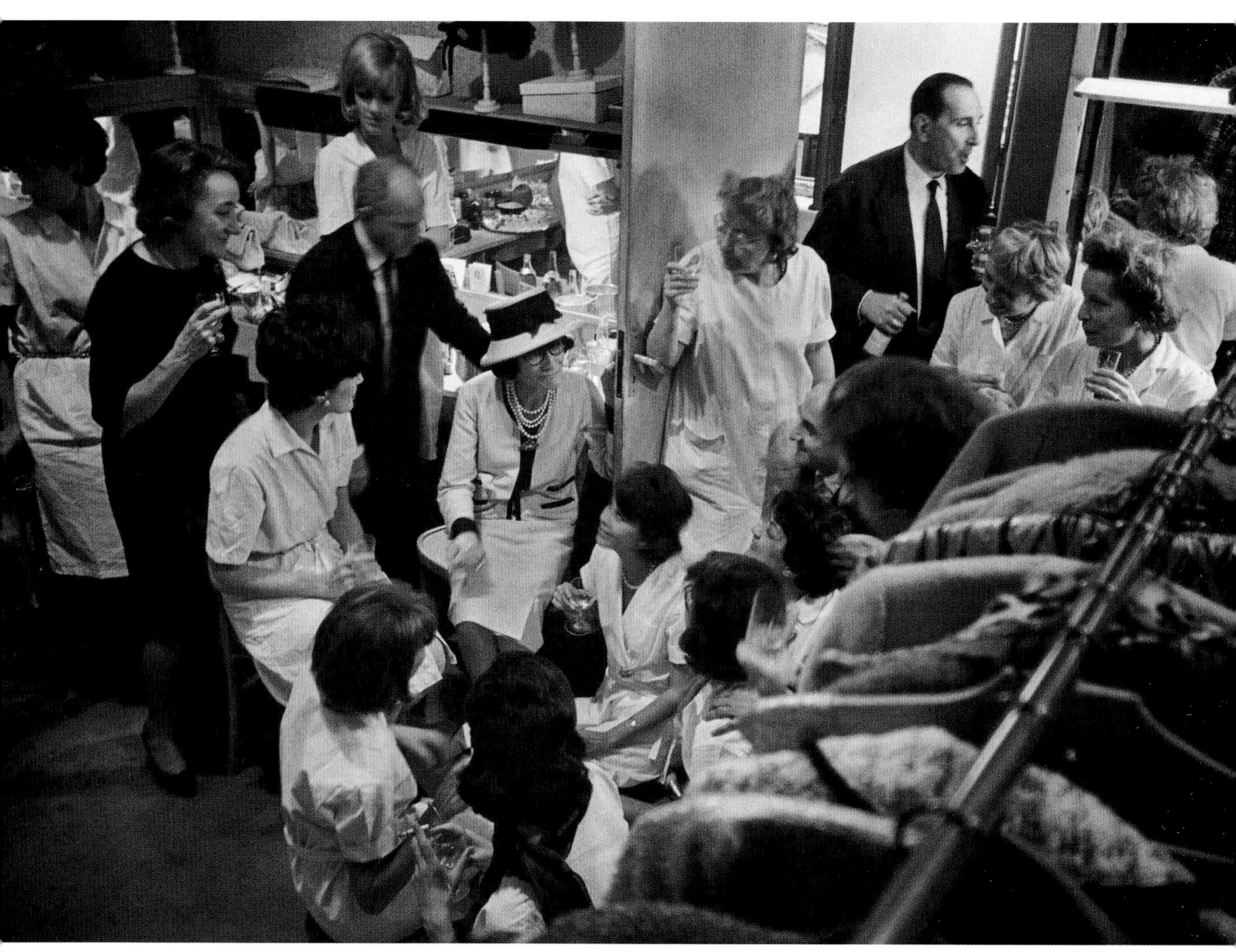

The celebration after the show, another spectacular success! "She still makes others look as if they tried too hard," said one fashion editor.

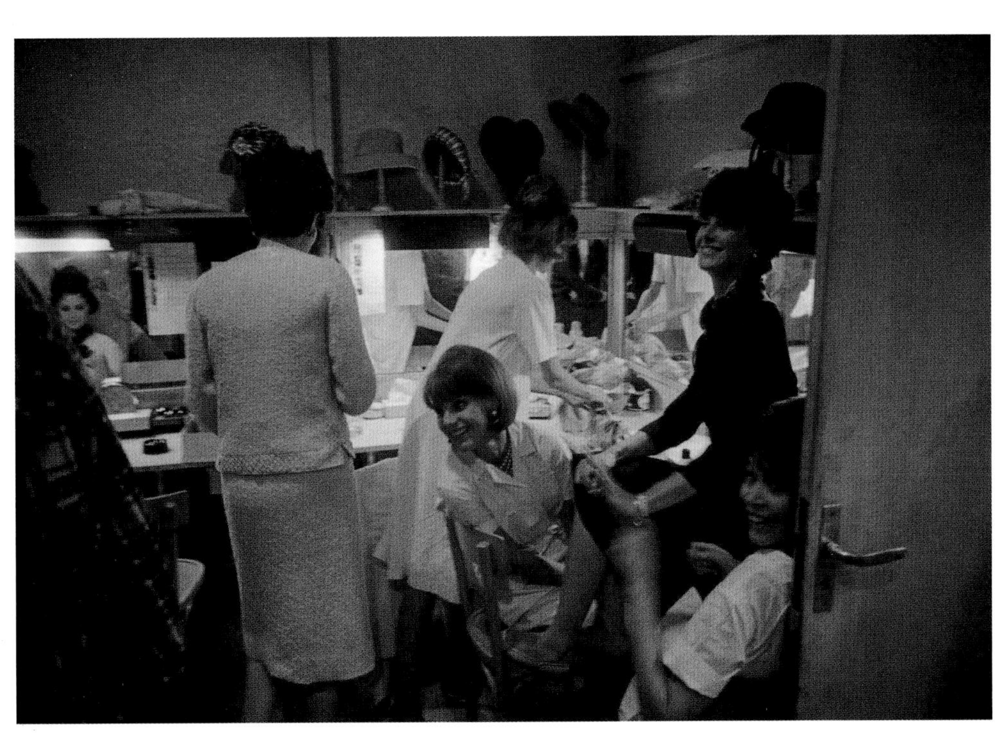

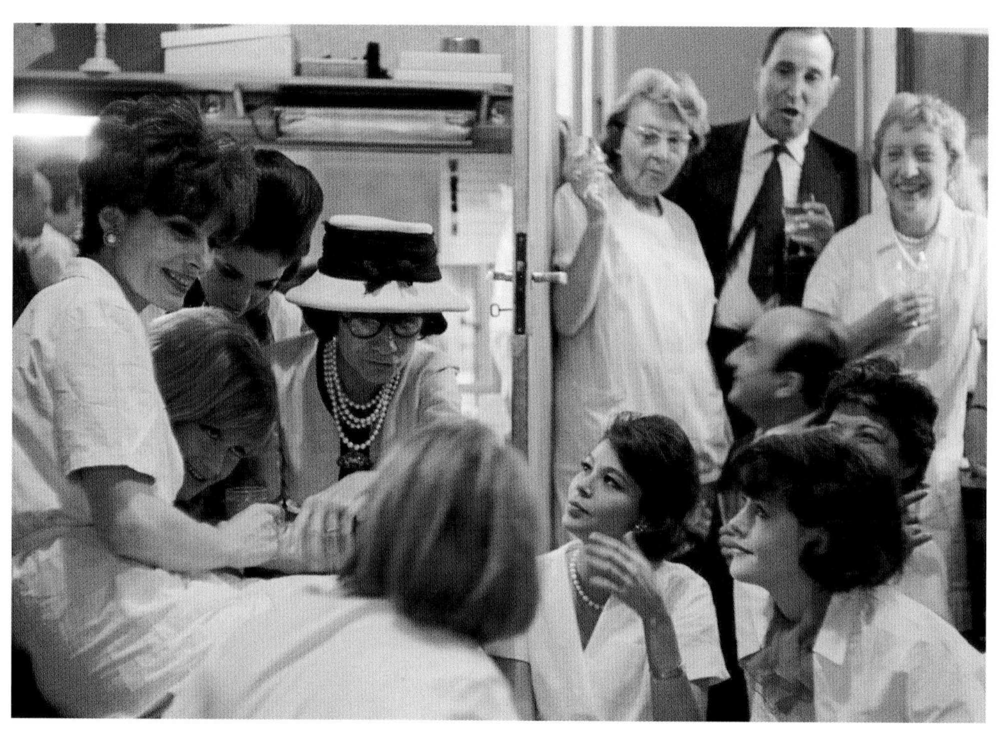

Mademoiselle loved to gossip with the girls and start intrigues.

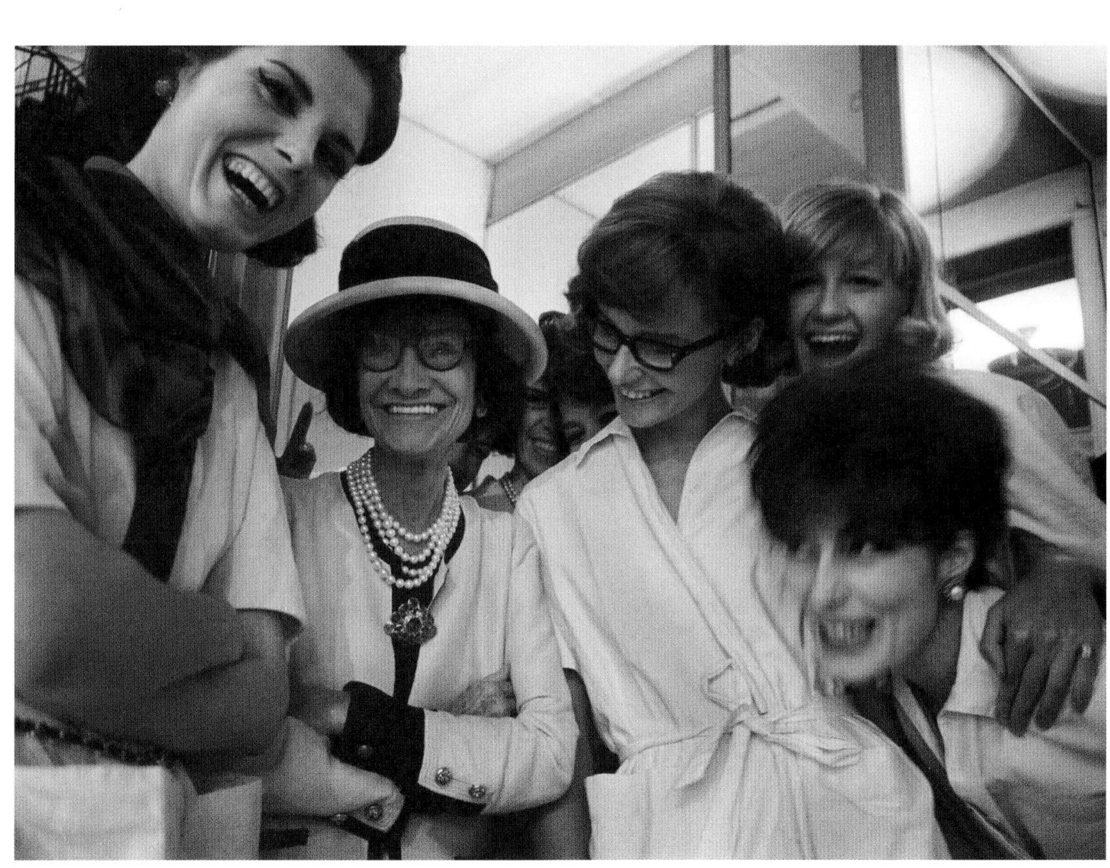

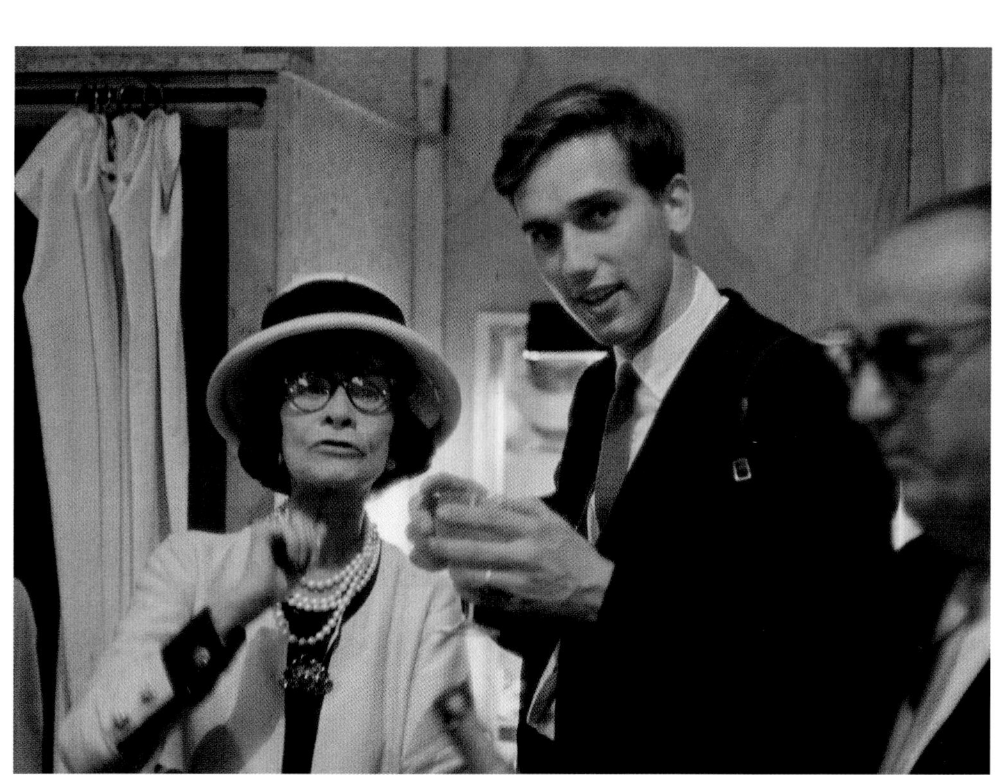

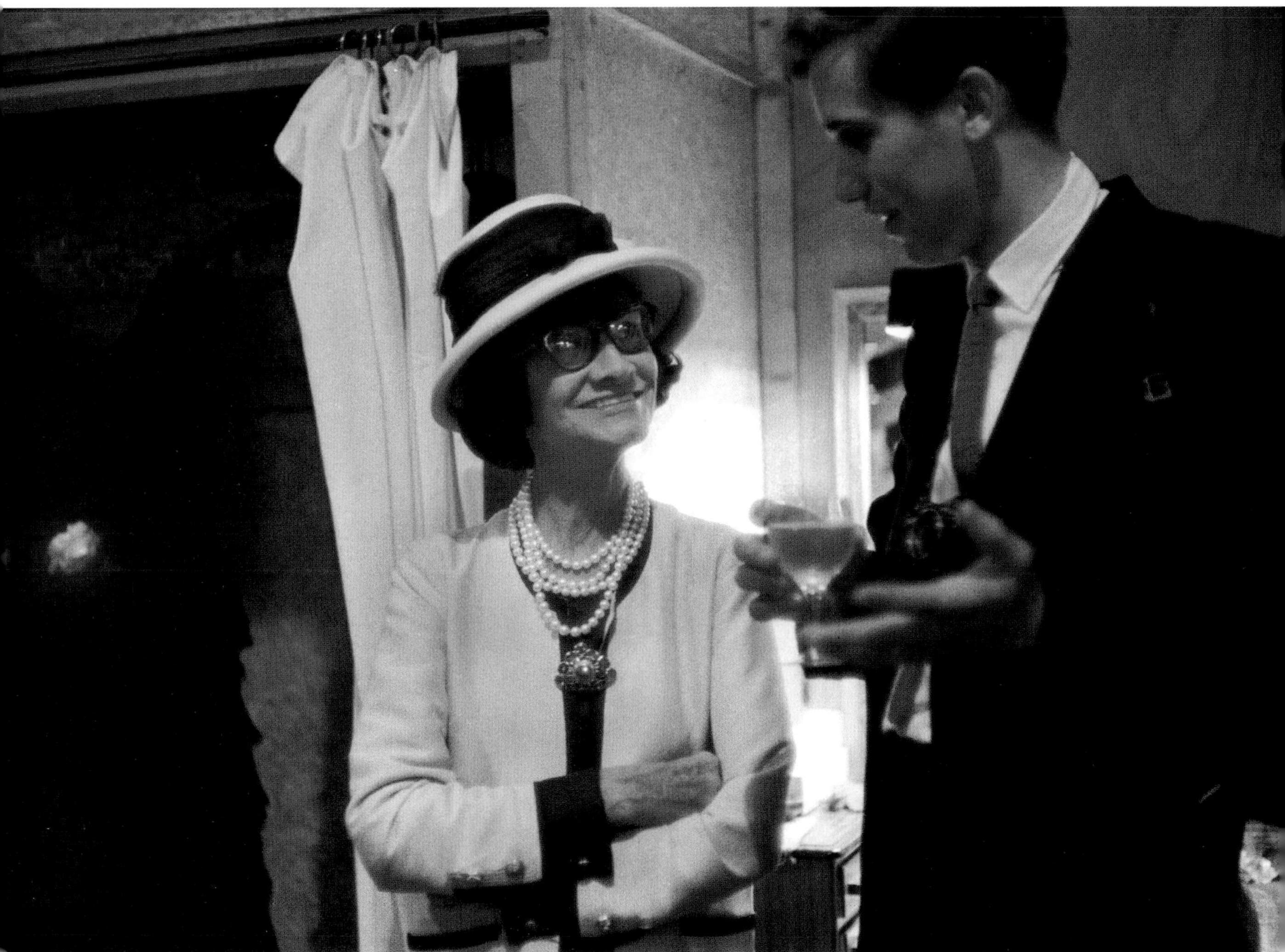

I invented my life by taking for granted that everything I did not like would have an opposite, which I would like.

*Coco*

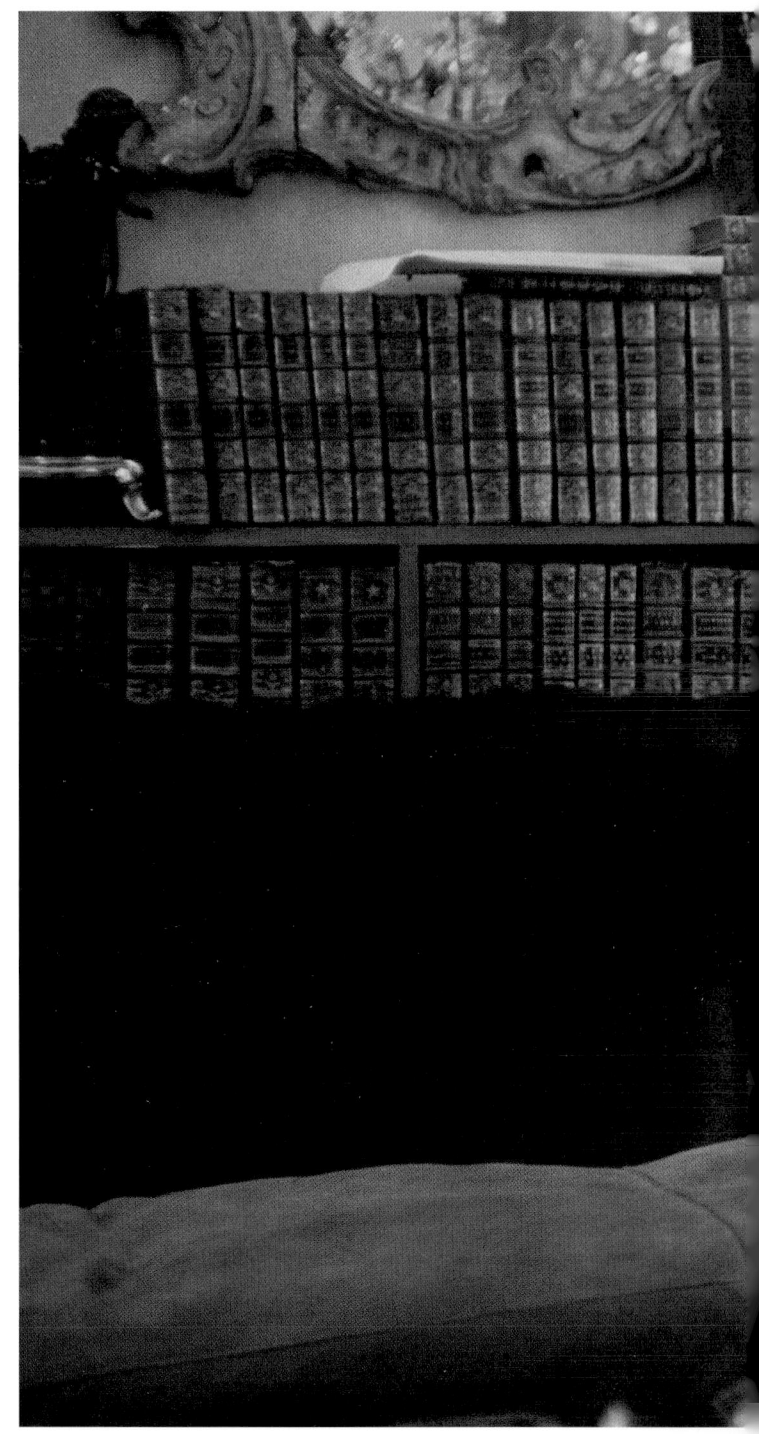

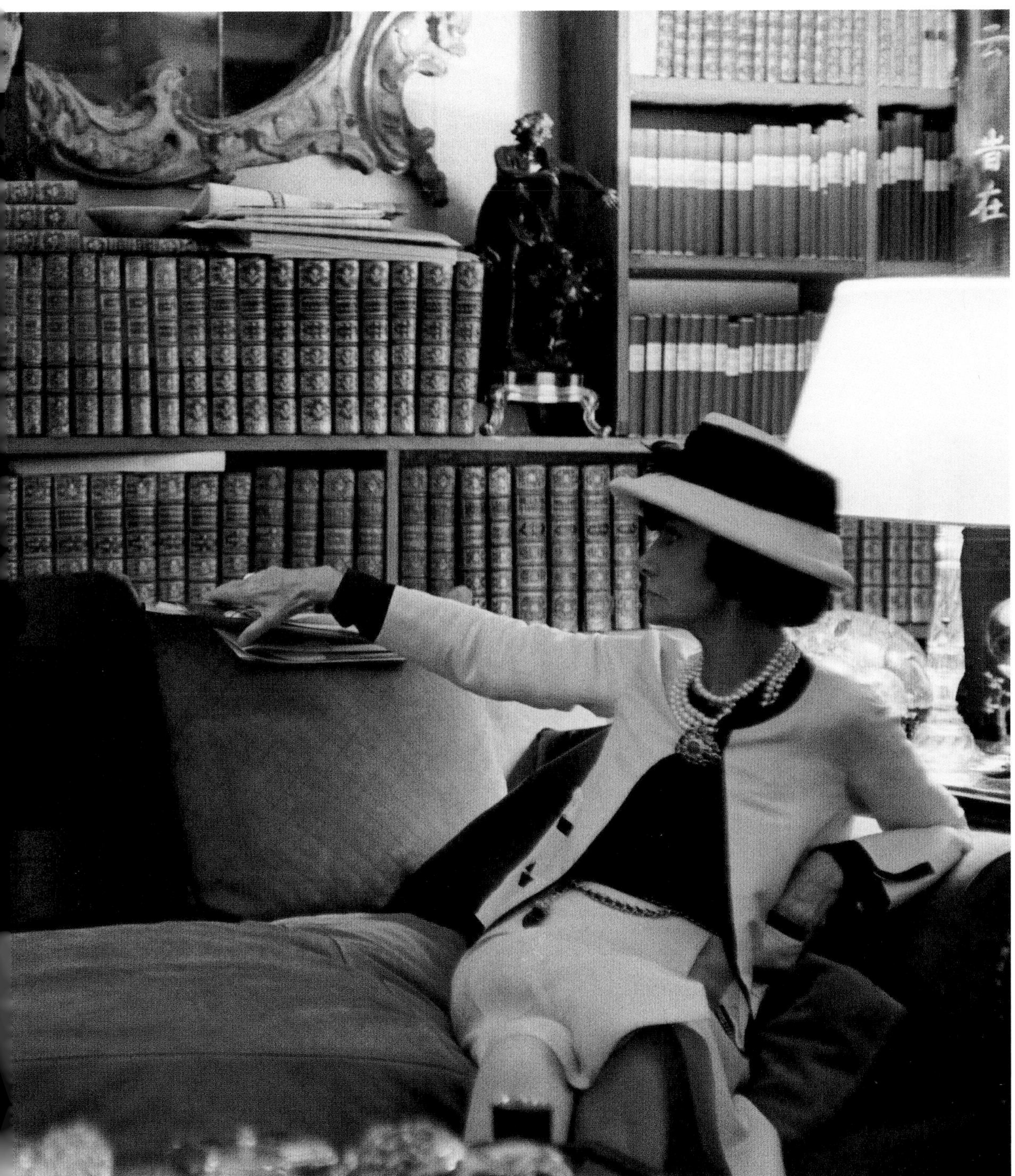

Mademoiselle made "junk" jewelry fashionable

and is wearing it mixed with $69,000 pearls.

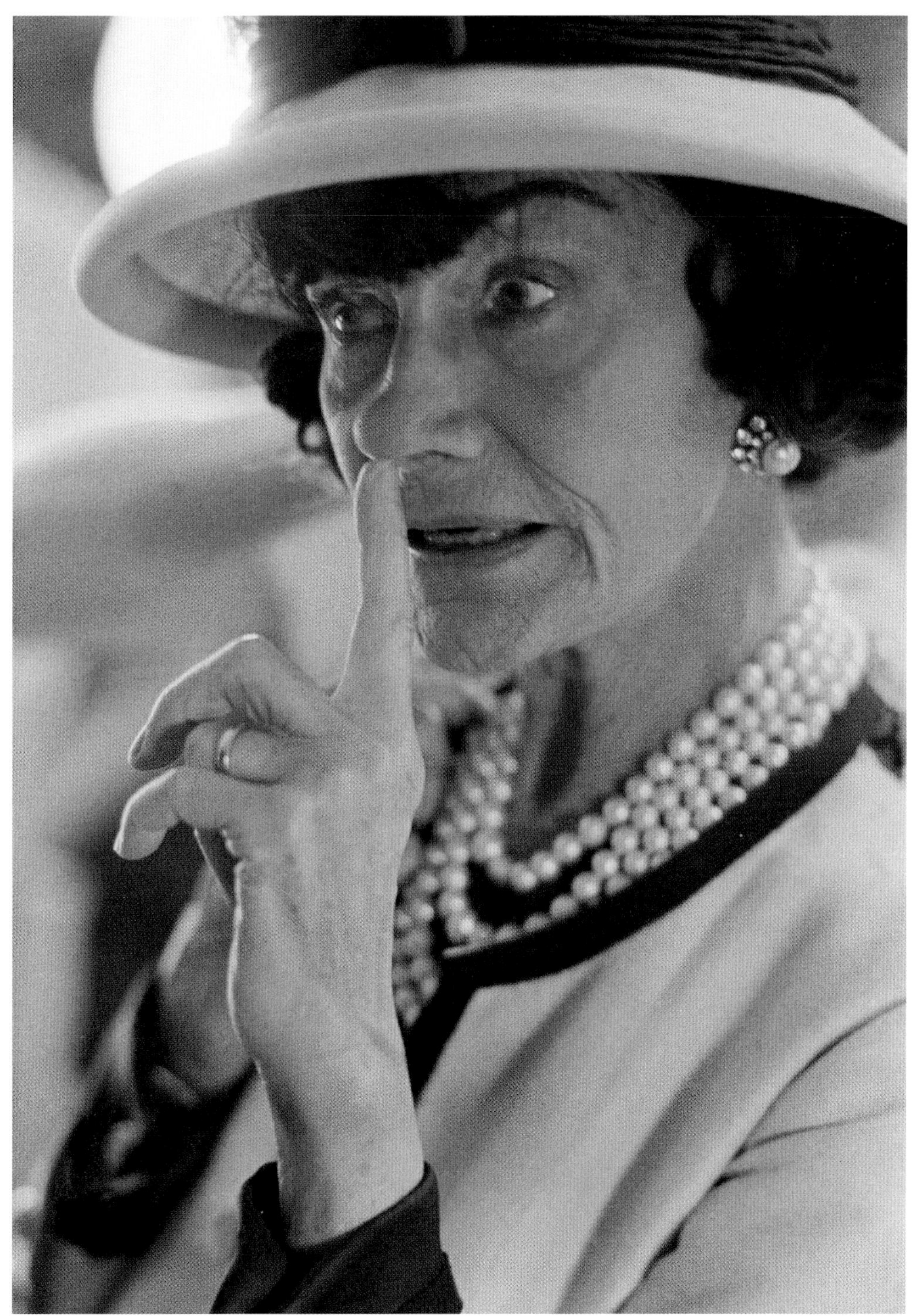

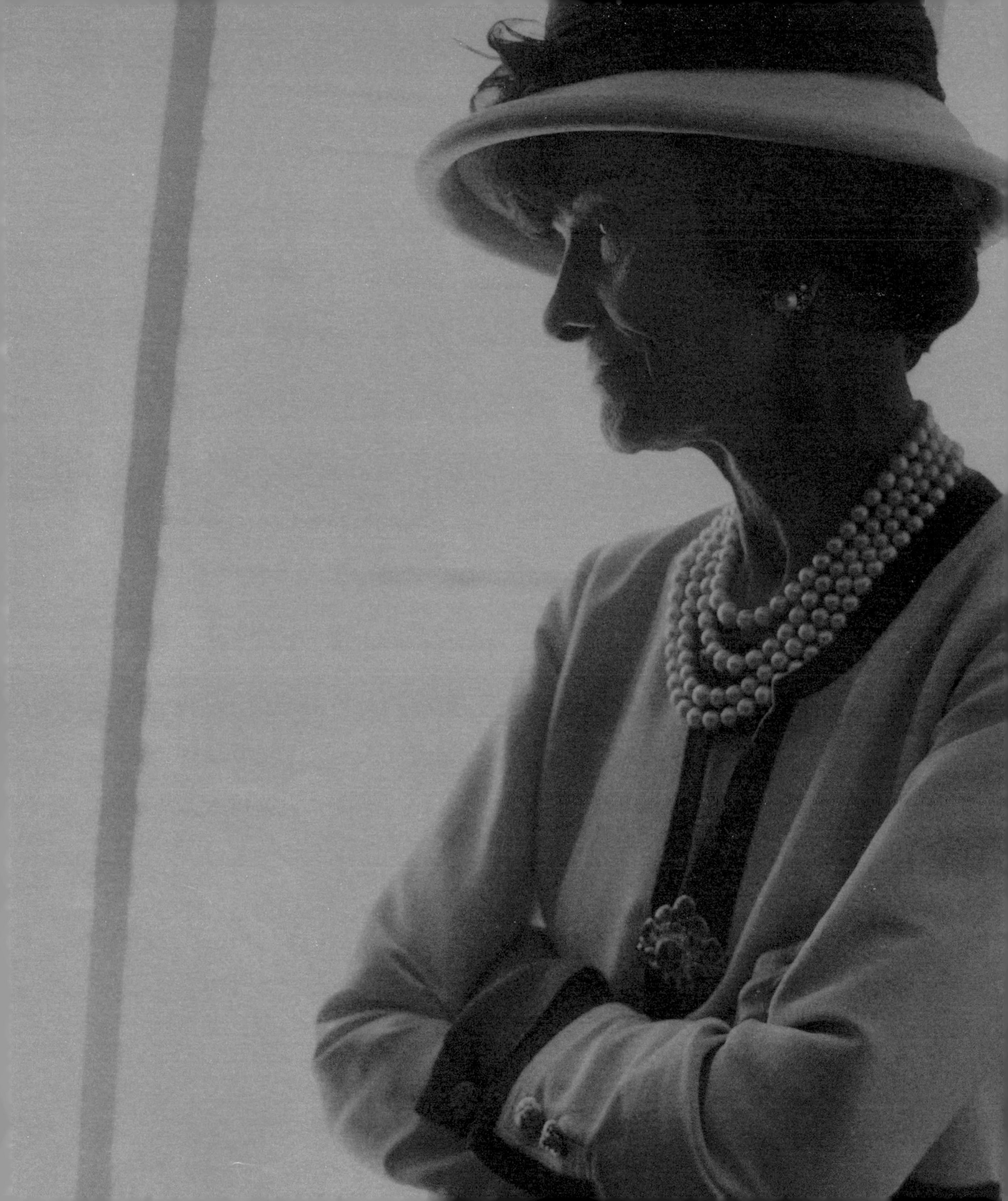

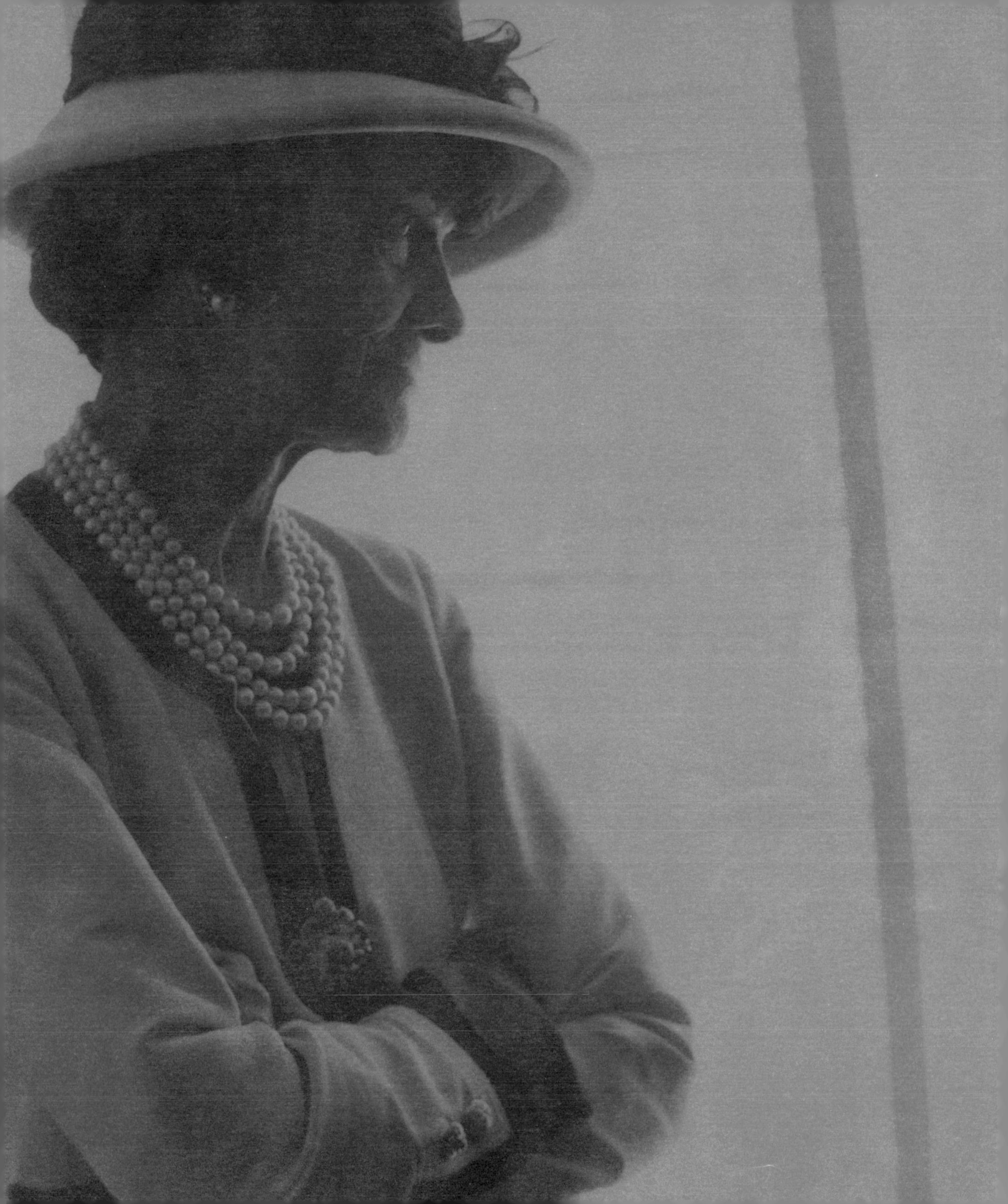

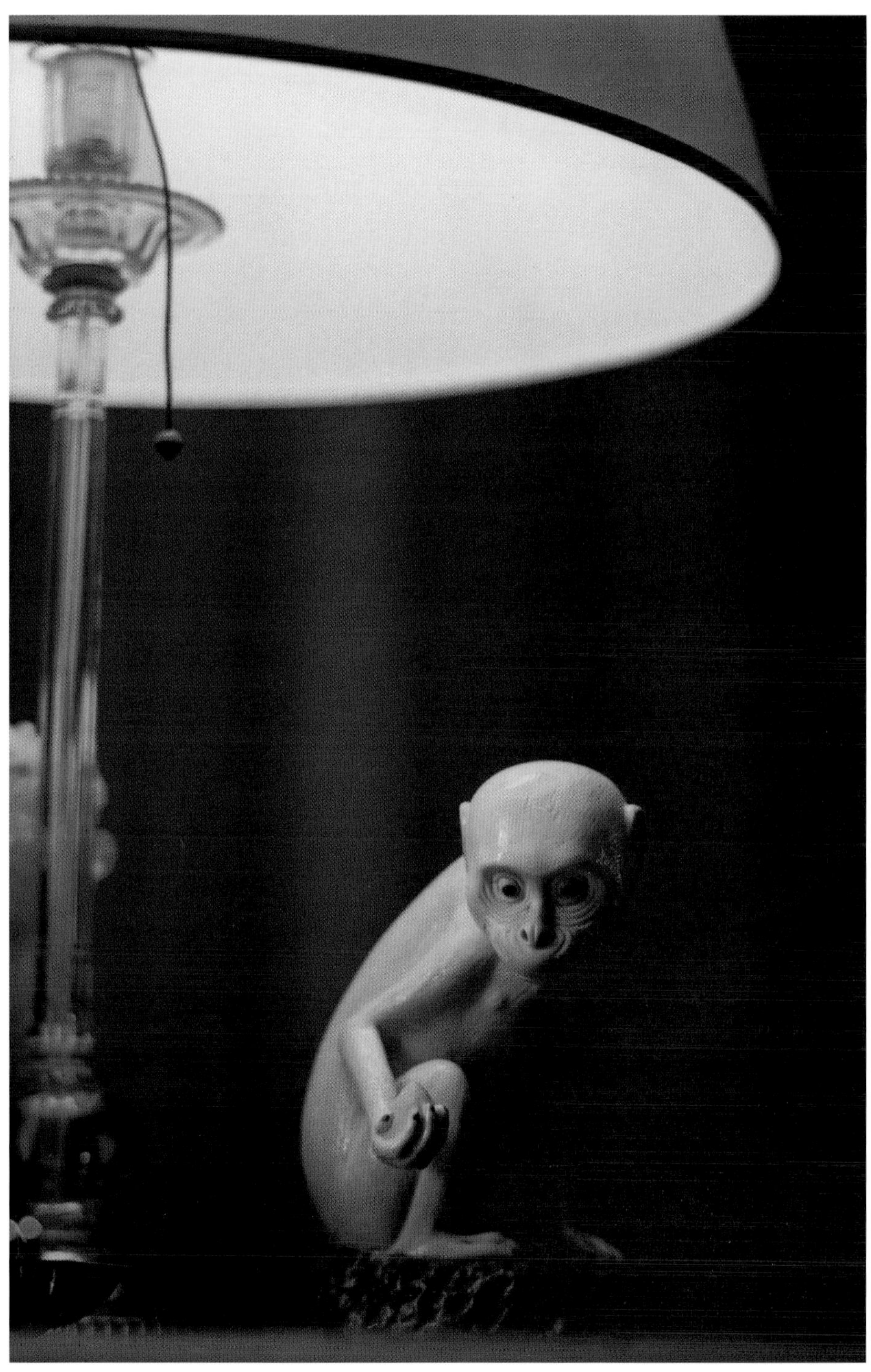

This monkey, Mademoiselle mischievously said, reminded her of Richard Avedon.

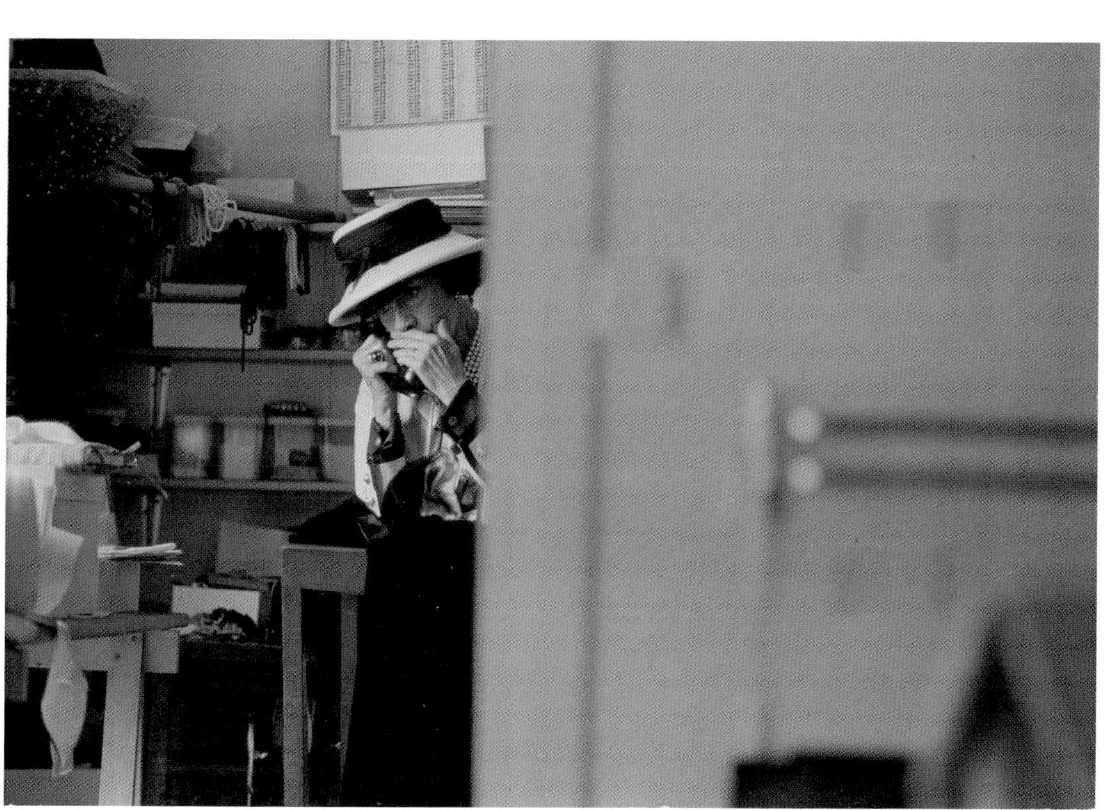

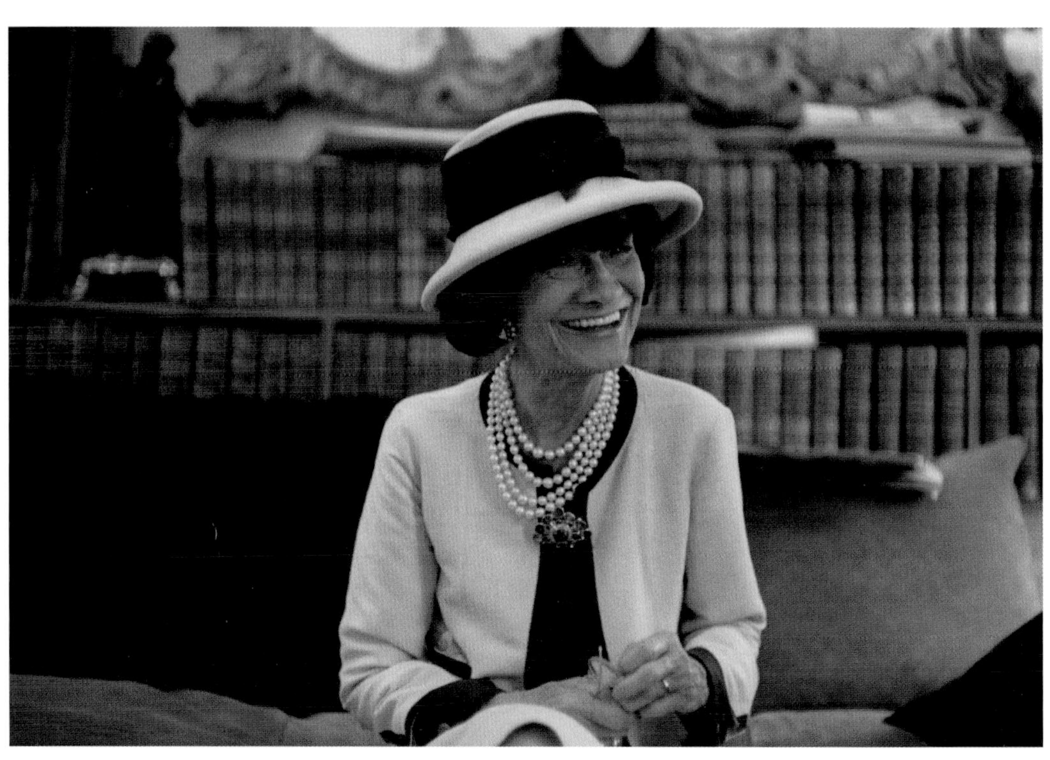

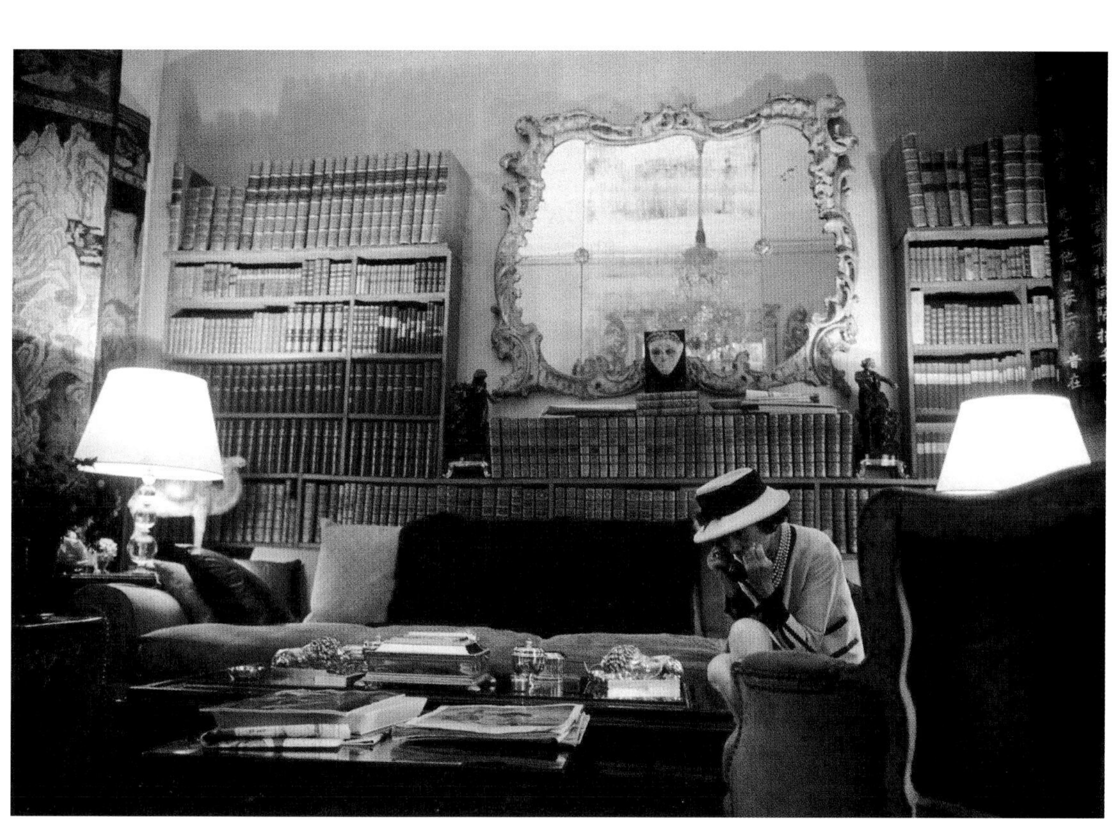

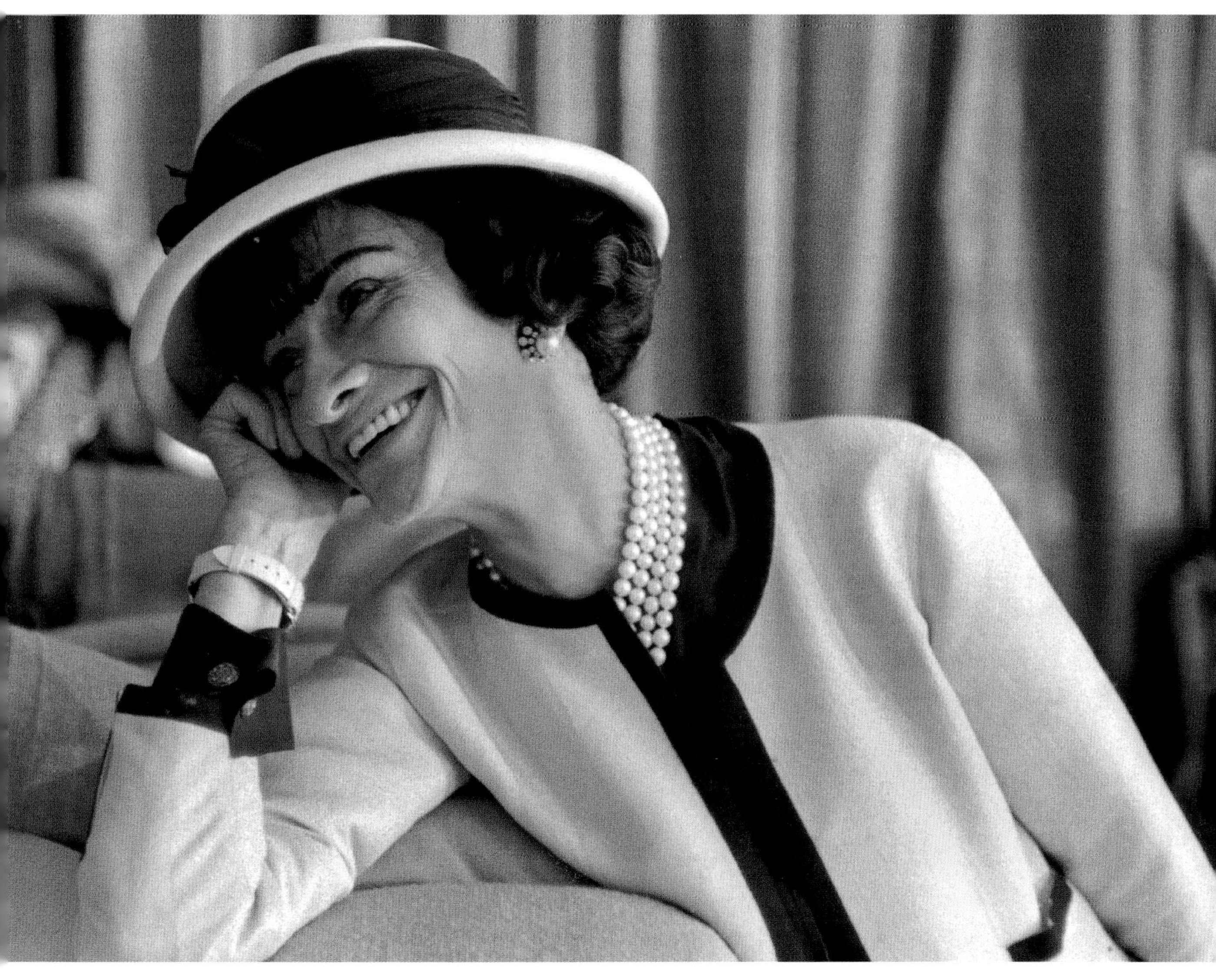

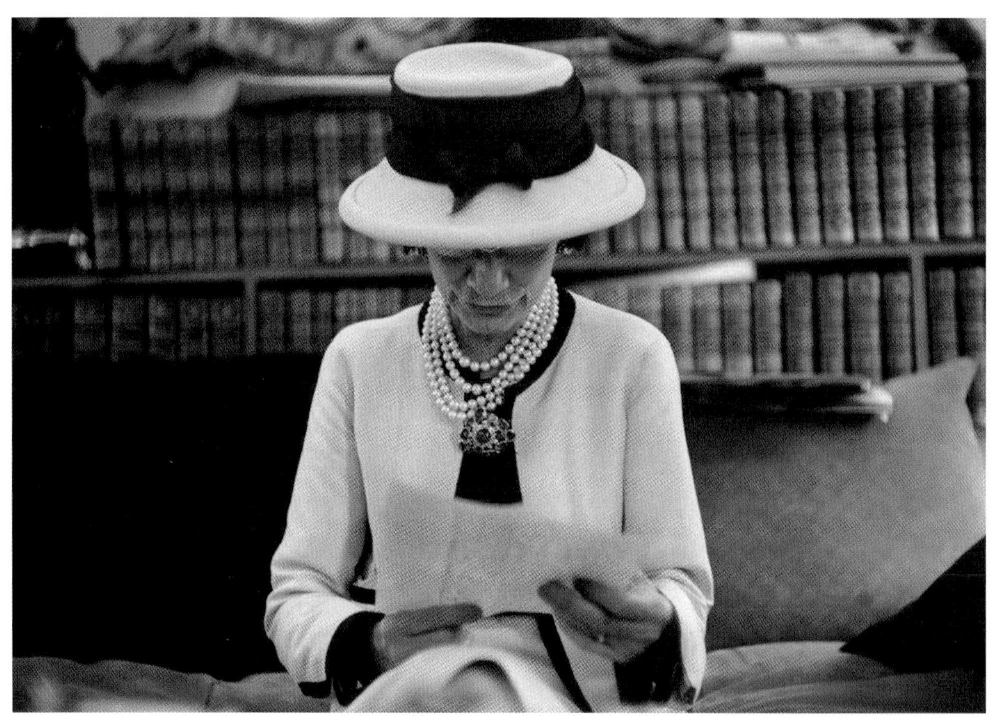

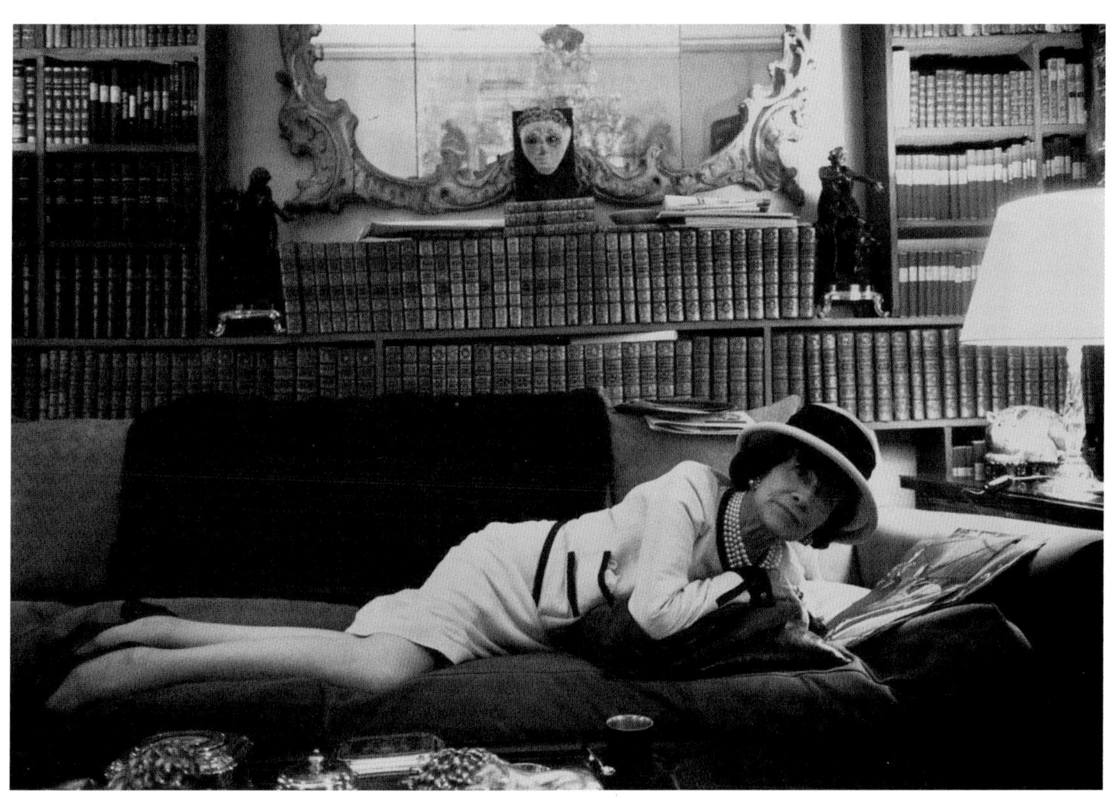

Chanel demonstrates her favorite restful pose. Her legs are those of a young woman.

You can be gorgeous at twenty, charming at forty,
and irresistible for the rest of your life.

As we left for Versailles that Saturday afternoon, Mademoiselle wore one of her most famous accessories, the Chanel sunglasses.

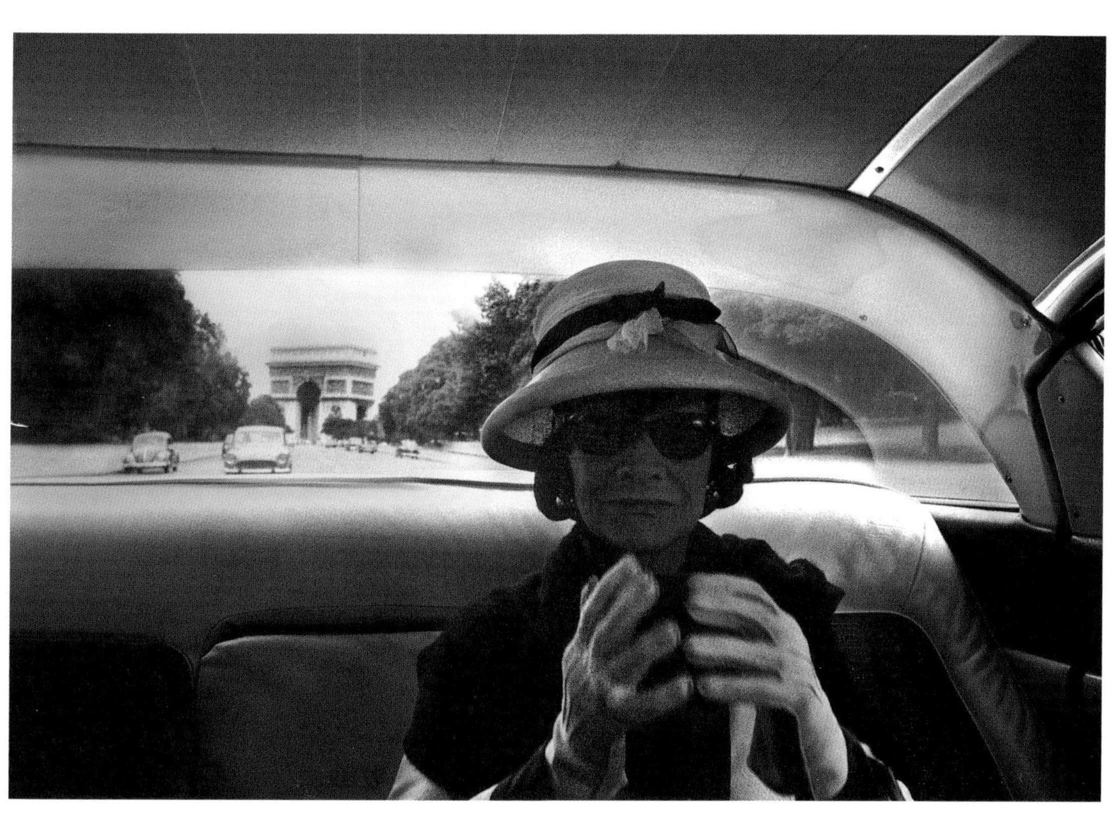

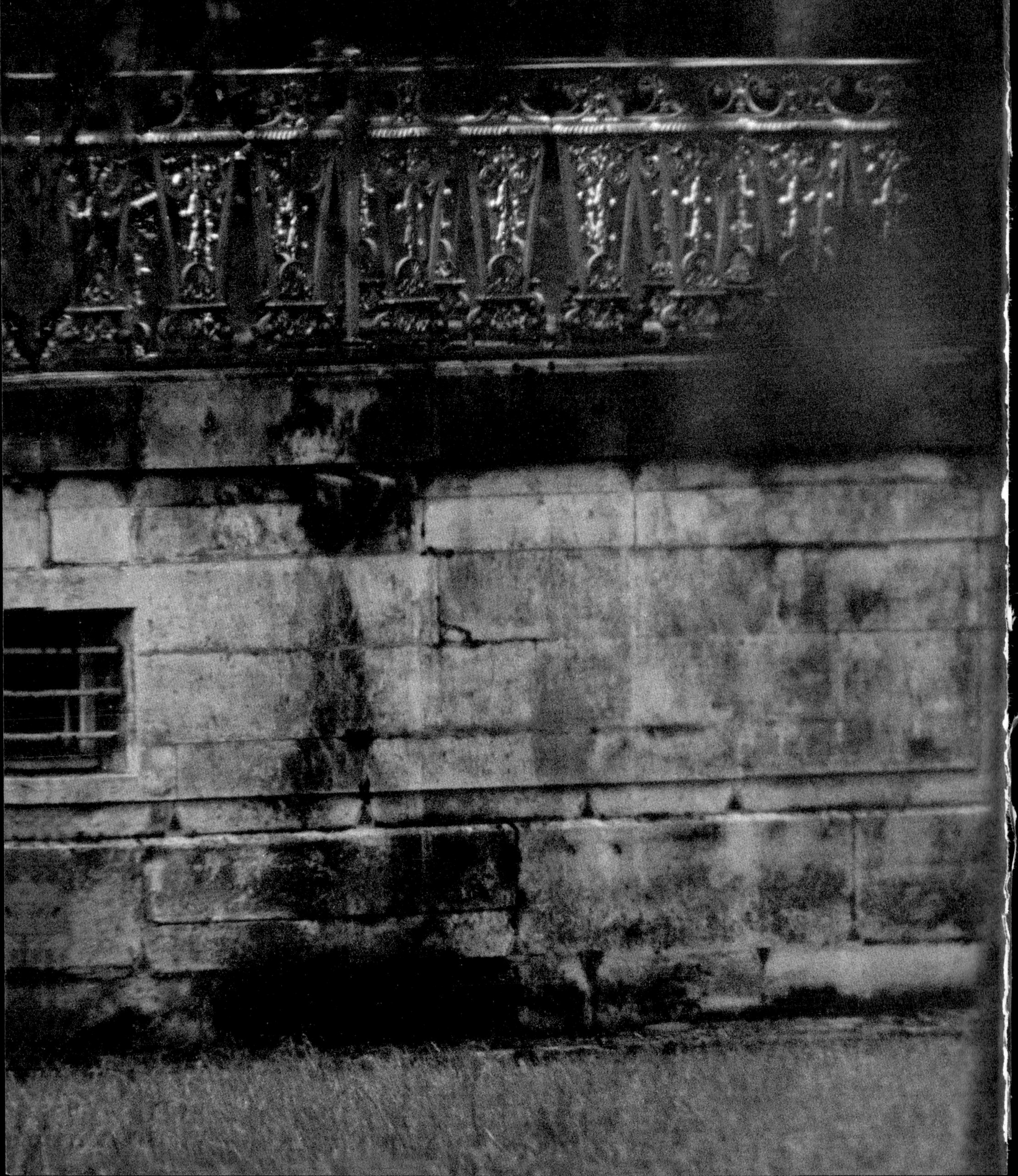

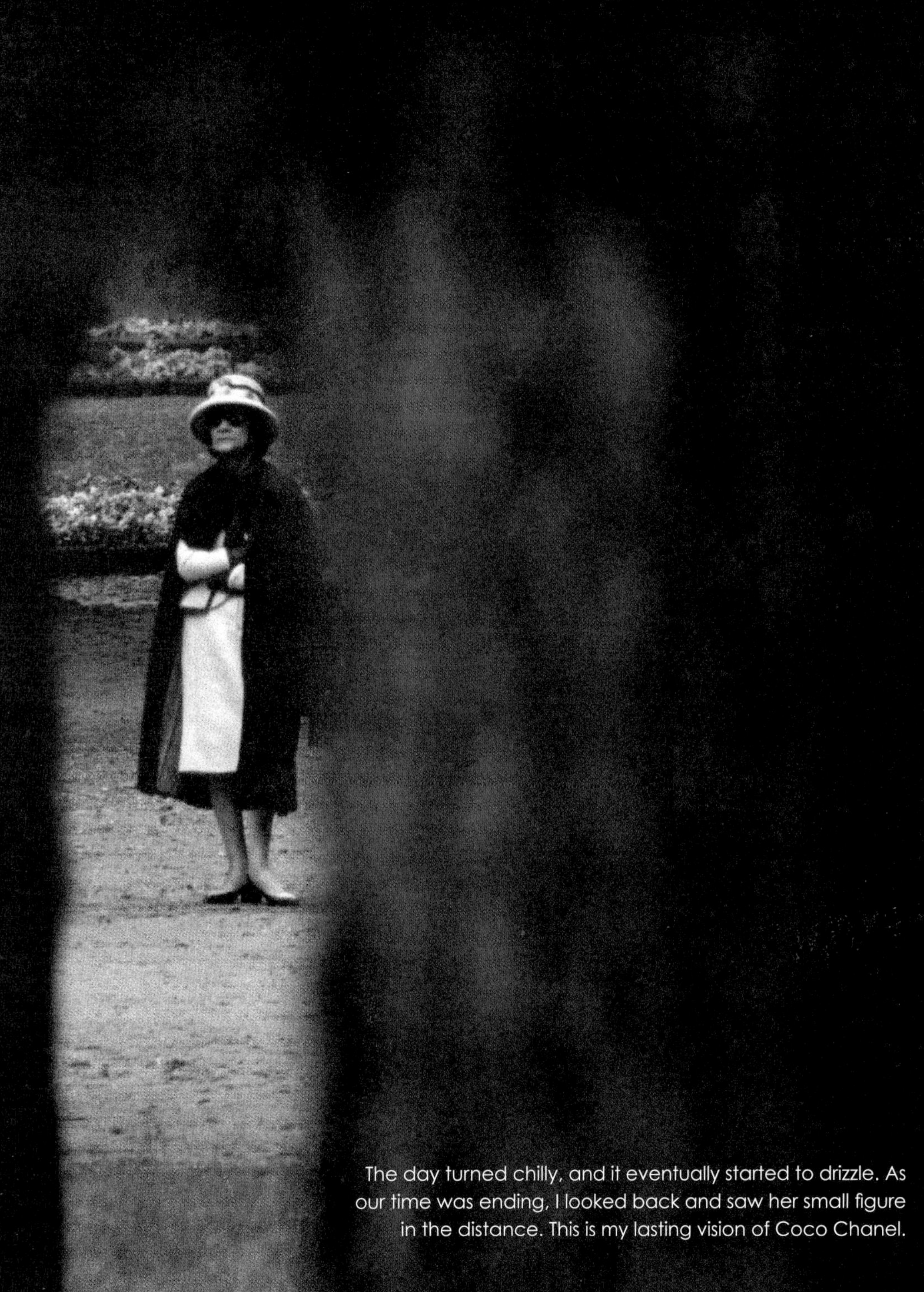

The day turned chilly, and it eventually started to drizzle. As our time was ending, I looked back and saw her small figure in the distance. This is my lasting vision of Coco Chanel.

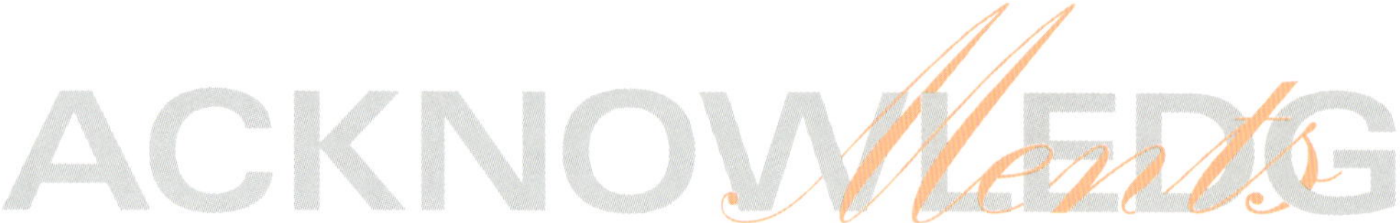


This book could not have happened without the help and contributions of these great women:

Thank you, Marta Hallett, my dynamic publisher, who never fails to see beyond the horizon; Sarah Morgan Karp, who designed this book with sensitivity, elegance, and taste; and Signe Bergstrom.

My gratitude goes to my friends, the brilliant Judith Thurman for her insightful foreword, and Nancy Griffin, who has always been prepared to edit my words when I need her most.

This book could never have happened without my very special Françoise, my life's love, always enthusiastically pressing forward with tireless dedication and devotion.

And my supreme teacher: Coco Chanel. Merci Mademoiselle! Thank you also to our family and friends.

I also want to acknowledge and thank our very special elves Miranda Brackett and Will Thoren, who always kept things running smoothly; Imacon scanners; HP printers; Canon Cameras; and the Eastman Kodak Company.